July 2022

Dig DEEP

Exceeding Your Potential

Philip M. Bonaparte II

Copyright © 2016 by Philip M. Bonaparte II

Dig DEEP
Exceeding Your Potential
by Philip M. Bonaparte II

Printed in the United States of America

ISBN 9781498463171

All rights reserved solely by the author. The author guarantees all contents are original and do not infringe upon the legal rights of any other person or work. No part of this book may be reproduced in any form without the permission of the author. The views expressed in this book are not necessarily those of the publisher.

Unless otherwise indicated, scripture quotations are taken from The New King James Version (NKJV). Copyright 1979, 1980, 1982 by Thomas Nelson, Inc. Used by permission. All rights reserved.

www.xulonpress.com

Dedication

To my mother and father for raising me,
To D-Ray for training me,
To my family and friends for believing in me,
And to my grandmother for disciplining me every way possible.

Acknowledgments

First and foremost, I have to thank God for who he is and what he continues to do in my life. This book has landed in your lap because of Him and that is not something that I take lightly. God is the creator of the universe, but He still takes the time to love on a crazy kid from Jersey like me. He ordered my steps from before I was even born in order to have the life lessons necessary to produce this book.

Next, I must thank my family and "friends". I say friends to separate those that can't get rid of me due to the blood running through their veins and those that can't get rid of me because I just won't let them. All of those that are close to me know that we are not friends, but family. I thank my father and mother for always encouraging and supporting me. I want to thank my sisters, Philicia and Shantay, for being the pain-in-the-necks that I cannot live without. Our relationship is unique and I wouldn't trade it for the world. My extended family, with my grandmother as the head, are always great parts of my life when we come together and I love you all dearly.

I cannot forget my brothers and sisters from Lee University (you know who you are) and more specifically, the Voices of Lee. We have had great times together and those memories taught me more than I could have ever imagined. Who says you can't have fun and learn at the same time?

As you will soon see from reading this book, I am a firm believer that everything that happens in one's life has a purpose to it. With that being said, I want to also thank every person that I have run into throughout my life. Whether friend or foe, around for my failures or success (or both), a person that took the time to greet me in passing or someone that I will hold dear forever, your life has had a purpose in mine and I am truly grateful for it.

Table of Contents

Introduction: Changing Your You xi
Chapter 1: Digging for Purpose.................................... 15
Chapter 2: Reactive or Proactive? 23
Chapter 3: Why do People Fail to
   Discover Their Purpose?.............................34
Chapter 4: The Why 45
Chapter 5: L.O.V.E. 56
Chapter 6: Creating Your Purpose Statement 65
Chapter 7: Doubt 77
Chapter 8: Self-Doubt 86
Chapter 9: Societal Doubt...97
Chapter 10: Facing & Confronting
   Doubts 107
Chapter 11: Excuses 115
Chapter 12: The Threshold 130
Chapter 13: Engagement 143
Chapter 14: Stability and Success..............................154
Chapter 15: Performance:
   Significance 162
Chapter 16: Following Up and Opening Up 203
Conclusion: Resting and
   Maintaining..215

Introduction

Changing Your You

"I don't know what to do" I said to myself. With my back flat on the bed for me to stare into the darkness surrounding me, I noticed how the imagery also represented where I was in life. It was my senior year in college and I did not know what to do next. My time at the university seemed meaningless because what I believed I needed to get out of it continued to elude me. I must have ran around in my mind for hours to discover whatever it is I needed to put me at rest. I was blind to what the future held and uncertain of what it would bring. My fear and confusion brought me to a place of isolation. I was numb. My heart sank deeper into my chest to, what I thought, hide itself from the pain of emptiness.

What happened to me that evening brought me to a point that I never want to go back to. As my grandmother would say, I was "sick and tired of being sick and tired". My heart sunk into my chest not to hide, but to go in and discover the greatness that has always been within me. It went digging for its purpose and to bring forth the light that is to shine for the world. Once I discovered this, I wanted to help others that are dealing with the same thing. This is where this book comes form. Now do not expect to just read this book because it was not designed for that. You will NOT get the most out of it in that manner. There needs to be interaction. Highlight things. Take notes. Go back and reference the information. Place quotes and responses on your walls and mirrors; write it on your forehead if you have to. Start implementing things into your daily routine and always dig a little deeper into your character so it can translate into your actions. Information is pointless if it is not put into action so let's make it happen cap'n! You will notice that I am a bit eccentric at times and come up with some crazy analogies, but if you can laugh with me then you can also cry and that's what I want. I want this to be used as a diving board into the depths of your soul as you discover the beauty that has been within you all this time. There is a plethora of colors and life that go far and beyond anything you can imagine when just at the surface. It takes the experience of going deep down in the midst to truly understand its greatness. Your greatness:

The gift is passion. The talent is perseverance. The goal is change. The outcome is consistency. They render their best simply because it is their best. No one has to say anything and nothing must happen in order for the magic to come alive. The only thought is how to make things better. People, places, organizations, genres, styles, ideas, and thoughts are all part of the puzzle. There is no hope that it can happen, only the will to make it happen. Imagination and creativity are parts of the birthright they have decided to use as catalysts for innovation and change.

Some may call them different, others call them insane. To do the same thing and expect a different result is the true rendition of such an accusation, and contrast from the norm is what makes the inception of what others say is impossible so beautiful. It is only after the dawn the world is capable of seeing how radiant and warm the light of tomorrow is. By then, these people have already become the heroes and symbols of greatness.

They are one of a kind, but they feel they are simply doing what they were born to do. They discovered their purpose, they pursued it with tenacity, and they made what was once a dream, reality.

Time is the only thing that separates science fiction from science fact. Doubts and excuses are the only things that have ever destroyed a prosperous future. Engagement in one's purpose is the first step to have it consume you and, eventually, get you to perform at a level you did not even know was possible. To let something consume you, to really let go and take the risk that is as specific to you as your fingerprint is how you change your situation. That is how you change the world. That is how you change, you.

Dig deep within yourself to find what has been covering the better you. Dig deep to uncover the "you" that you were born to be. Dig deep to discover who you are meant to be and start from there. It is only when you work from the end that you get to the end. And the work starts now.

A smile is on my face because I am excited to see what each of us can do; what each of us will do. So, shall we begin to dig?

Chapter 1

Digging for Purpose

Like a tree, you must constantly focus on your roots growing as deep as your branches grow up and out to connect your inner-being to the outer world.

Before the turn of the 21st century, things like the internet and the CD-Rom were the new hot commodities that wow-ed the world and presented new ideas for the future. Now, people have internet access with their cell phones and CDs are almost obsolete (unless you like mini-Frisbees) as most information is just downloaded straight to any device. Merriam-Webster struggles to keep up with the new words being produced while we as consumers rush to purchase the hottest and newest commodity annually because things are constantly changing (and burning a hole in our wallets).

Just add water and you can eat a cup of noodles in under two minutes or make a frozen meal edible in under four. The demand in this age of information and knowledge is speed as we do not want it now, but *right now* as just about anything you purchase today will be out-of-date before you are in the confines of your home to appreciate it. This rapid rate of growth is hurting us more than it is helping us as the need for the progression of material things weaves itself into our personal lives.

Busier schedules and more time texting than talking face-to-face to another human being has led to the destruction of relationships. Individual finances are deteriorating due to our focus on

{True!}

wants and not needs. Purchasing things that we want now with the trendy credit card has led to universal turmoil as interest from these companies enslave us.

Relationships are empty because it is not about what we can put into them, but what we can get out. Climbing the corporate ladder is synonymous to running the rat race because employees are "easily replaceable" and you only "need" the position you are currently in. Everything is expanding around us and we ourselves try to do the same exact thing to keep up with the demand.

The world may be achieving a lot of things as a whole and reaching to the skies and broadening its horizon, but we are neglecting the importance of depth in our character.

Growth is nearly impossible as we play catch up with the unexpected expenses, sudden lay-offs, failed exams, and drama among family and friends that seem to be happening all at the same time! The world may be achieving a lot of things as a whole and reaching to the skies and broadening its horizon, but we are neglecting the importance of depth in our character. We have forgotten to create a foundation. We have lost the process of discovery within ourselves. We have abandoned our need for consistence and stern beliefs. We have given up our rights to think for ourselves and, most importantly, digging deep within ourselves.

To dig deep, you must slow things down and let it all sink in. You must scratch and claw for something that may take weeks, months or even years to find. You must focus on the process, not the production. You must define purpose and its importance to you. You begin to create your future with vision and action. You advocate change and prosperity by setting an example and emulating the proper characteristics necessary to achieve it. You become the independent variable in this interdependent world. You are in a constant phase of research and development so the depth inside correlates to the behavior outside.

Digging for Purpose

Overall, you must understand who you are, why you are here, and what you must do to achieve your purpose. Like a tree, you must constantly focus on your roots growing as deep as your branches grow up and out to connect your inner-being to the outer world. In order to do this, you must ask yourself the million-dollar question.

The Million-Dollar Question

Asking *why* is the first stage of bringing depth into any scenario and helps solve a lot of problems by shifting our focus to the right things.

A couple years ago, a group of my friends and I went out to dinner after being away from each other for a mighty long time. However, even as we were there, we were *not there*. We were physically in the restaurant, but our minds were someplace else. Each of us used our cell phones to reach to the outside world, connecting to people other than our dinner guests. As I noticed this, I asked myself the million-dollar question: W*hy*? Why were we even out together if we were going to just sit there and use our phones? Why even come? After asking myself that question about eating with my friends, I started to ask this question in *every* other area in my life. I began to realize that I was doing a lot of things without any purpose at all. A lot of my actions were habits created without thought and without focus. When you ask why, you are looking for purpose. Your curiosity leads to a better understanding, and inevitably you doing better on what you do and how you go about doing it. It brings clarity and focus by looking at the big picture first. Asking why is the first stage of bringing depth into any scenario and helps solve a lot of problems that we have by shifting our focus to the right things.

Defining Purpose

"The problem is not the problem. The problem is your attitude about the problem." (Captain Jack Sparrow)

Purpose, in its simplified description, is the reason something exists. As unique as a fingerprint, each person, moment, and group has a very specific and detailed purpose. A position within our past, present, and future designed to be the connection of all living things, leading to the unanimity of all things within the world (to begin the unsimplified description). Purpose is selfless and giving, but requires the in-depth knowledge of ourselves and our relation to society. Its desire is growth and the rendering of our very best in every aspect of our lives.

Although how we reach our purpose and what tools we use to produce its fruits may (and often) change, why we seek its success is usually the same throughout time. To search and go after one's purpose should be at the forefront of every life and action. It is built into our genetic makeup. When we and our actions lack purpose, a black hole forms within our very being, destroying us from the inside out. It hinders our progress and forces us to be in a place of confusion and pain.

I have encountered numerous people from all walks of life that have yet to discover their purpose (with me being the main one). I have found this leads to empty relationships, misconstrued goals, ineffective efforts, and in some cases lives that were almost put to ruin. You may find you have something in common with one or more of their stories.

I am living a life that most would consider successful as I excel in my profession and prosper financially, but I am not happy. My job is just a job and it causes me to dread every Monday morning. I know there is more to life than this, but I do not know how to find it.

My marriage is hitting rock bottom. The passion is gone. We say we love each other, but there isn't any feeling behind the words. Counseling and going on getaways gives us a boost, but only temporarily. We need something that will last the rest of our lives, together.

Every year I set goals and start off with a full head of steam, only to revert back to my old habits. I have a lot more in me to give, but I do not know how to get it out of me. After trying so many things for so long, I am beginning to think that what I thought was there, isn't.

My children are bright and have a lot of potential, but all they want to do is play around or do things that they know they should not be doing. I don't know how to make what I tell them sink in.

The success of my business relies on me and me alone. My employees don't take matters into their own hands and I feel as if they are only doing this for a paycheck. This is my life and I know that I must put in the effort, but I am losing my family, my friends, and myself in the process. I want what I put in to outlive my years. How do I get them to understand the vision I have for this company and reclaim my personal life?

I cannot remember the last time I have had a good night's rest. I struggle with not knowing what I am supposed to do next. I have done everything they have told me to do: go to college, get good grades, working as an intern and so forth. But, throughout this process, I have not discovered who I am. I could continue and get any "good" job and be miserable, but then what was the point of everything else?

All of these instances embed themselves deep within each of us by burying their negative influences into our spirits. We try to solve them with cookie-cutter solutions that only meet these issues on the surface. To deal with deep issues, we must dig deep within ourselves to discover the solution. In order to change our situation, we must first change ourselves. How do we do that? We change by looking within and discovering the answers to our problems. Change is first a thought, *then* an act. We must change our perception and shift our thinking and *then* we can change our actions and solve the problem. As Captain Jack Sparrow said, "The problem is not the problem. The problem is your attitude about the problem."

When we and our actions lack purpose, a black hole forms within our very being, destroying us from the inside out.

Kiddie Pool

It was Mother's Day and one thing I *must* do on Mother's Day is go to church with my mother for the Mother's Day Service because the woman who brought me in this world has the right to bring me out of it (and she would). It was there that I ran into a friend that I had not seen for quite some time. As we caught up, he told me how he might move to Colorado for work. I suggested we needed to go out on the town with the boys before he left.

He agreed and we started to talk about the stereotypical single young male things expected for a "night out on the town." The more we talked, the more ridiculous our planning got, but all in good fun and fiction. Although what we were coming up with was definitely creative, it was *highly* inappropriate (especially for church). As I agreed to be his wingman for this unlikely evening of endeavors, I asked him what type of girl he was interested in so I knew what to look for.

He cut me off and said, "No worries about that man. I am like a kiddie pool, extremely shallow."

We both cackled at the visual, but I also put a lot of thought into it. The pace that we move in today forces us to look at things at a very simplified and basic level. Our choices and actions are often made impulsively due to our lack of purpose. When we are purposeful in what we do, we define our choices and our actions. They become focused just as they are designed to be. We overcome our shallow kiddie pool thinking by having a deep understanding of ourselves.

You must define who you are, what you are here to do, and how you will go about doing it.

Digging for Purpose

Key Points

- Like a tree, you must constantly focus on your roots growing as deep as your branches grow up and out to connect your inner-being to the outer world.
- The world may be achieving a lot of things as a whole and reaching to the skies and broadening its horizon, but we are neglecting the importance of depth in our character.
- Asking *why* is the first stage of bringing depth into any scenario, and helps solve a lot of problems by shifting our focus to the right things.
- "The problem is not the problem. The problem is your attitude about the problem," said Captain Jack Sparrow.
- When we and our actions lack purpose, a black hole forms within our very being, destroying us from the inside out.
- You must define who you are, what you are here to do, and how you will go about doing it.

Digging Deeper

At the end of each chapter there will be an opportunity for you to begin to implement the principles given in your own life. Take the time to go through this brief interactive section as you dig deeper into who you really are and what you are capable of doing.

Begin by asking yourself some probing questions.

Note: You cannot use your job title or academic rating to answer these questions.

- o *Who am I?*
- o *Why am I here?*
- ⊕ *What must I do to achieve my purpose?*
- o *Am I constantly focusing growing my roots deeper as my branches grow up or am I becoming top heavy?*

Note: a top heavy tree cannot withstand the storms of life!

When our actions lack purpose, a black hole forms within our very being, destroying us from the inside out. It hinders progress and forces us to be in a place of confusion and pain.

Is lack of purpose hindering your progress?

Are you living in a place of confusion and pain?

Reread the cases of lives that were almost put to ruin. *Did you find one or more that sounds like your life?* Explain your answer:

Are you ready to dig deep within yourself to discover the solution?

In order to change your situation, you must first change yourself. Change is first a thought, then an act. You must change your perception and shift your thinking.

Are you ready to define who you are, what you are here to do, and how you will go about doing it?

Chapter 2

Reactive or Proactive?

When you focus on the physiological, you become dependent on what happens to you and become a victim to everyone and everything around you.

For most of us, our focus in life has been completely opposite to what we are speaking of at this moment, and rightfully so. The reputable Maslow's Hierarchy of Needs is one that we all not only know from our education in school, but also in the lessons we are taught in life. We are taught that our natural needs are to be the focal point of our decisions. Although it is vital (no pun intended) to keep our physical bodies intact, there is a much more important part that is often forgotten and placed on the bottom of this totem pole called life.

Physiological, emotional, and spiritual are the three main groups that need to be met throughout our lives. *Physiological needs* are those things that, when effected, are obvious. In Maslow's chart, this would be the bottom two tiers rightfully named physiological (food, water, sex, sleep, oxygen, homeostasis, excretion) and security (of the body, employment, resources, morality, family, health, property).

As an infant, our physiological needs are our top priority. No matter what the circumstances are, it is *all about me*. We cry when we are thirsty, hungry, and tired. We groan when we want to be held or are feeling sick. This is expected from someone only a few years old, but why is it that we act the same decades later? We all have had a few (if not all) of these physiological thoughts in our minds one time or another. I know I have.

I am too tired to focus on this project right now. I will deal with it later.

Why is it that we have been sitting here all this time without anything to eat?

If I get hired to this company then I will not ever have to worry about working anyplace else. Most of their employees stay around for years.

All I need is this paycheck to pay my bills. I do not care about anything else.

I snapped at them because they snapped at me first! I must defend myself.

I am going out with him or her because I do not want to feel alone. I enjoy the security of having someone.

Do not misunderstand me, survival is important, but when you focus on the physiological, you become dependent on what happens to you. Essentially you become a victim to everyone and everything around you. You are re-active, not pro-active. Whenever life challenges you, you succumb to its hands of power and control by allowing it to be the basis of your actions.

When I was in school, my thought process was physiological all the way. The only things I worried about was having enough money to live, getting good enough grades to graduate, and keeping out (or just not being caught in) too much trouble that could get me expelled or thrown in jail. That just-enough or just-in-time mentality led to a very baseline and mediocre life for me.

On the outside, I had plenty of funds as I lived in a house and had my own vehicle and never went without. My grades could have been better, but I could have still squeezed a four-year degree into five. (Some of you will catch that a few phrases down). Although I had a few scares, trouble seemed to be more of a private issue than public. This would have been great for some, but it was awful for me. There were restless nights and moments of confusion and sadness because I knew there was more for me, but my stinkin' thinkin' kept me away from it. My physiological focus on the bare minimum, focusing on the short-term, and reacting to my situations was the gap between me and my purpose.

When you are re-active, not pro-active then whenever life challenges you, you succumb to its hands of power and control by allowing it to be the basis of your actions.

Emotional Needs

When you are focused not only on your needs but the way others perceive those needs, you are now in a stage of codependence.

The next two levels of Maslow's hierarchy involve the emotional needs of people. They are love/belonging (friendship, family, sexual intimacy), and esteem (self-esteem, confidence, achievement, respect of others, respected by others). When you are focused not only on your needs but the way others perceive those needs, you are now in a stage of codependence. Similarly to a toddler, your actions are based on how you react to a situation *along with* the reaction of others.

For instance, there was this funny video I saw on the internet one day of this baby that was intentionally falling *and* crying in order to get attention from family members. As the parent would walk down the hall and away from the child, the child would get up, get in sight of the parent, fall and cry. Codependence focuses on how you feel emotionally, but that emotion is still dependent on another factor. In most cases, that factor is how others or things react to you. Codependence sounds a lot like this.

I cannot do that because if I did, my mother would kill me!

If I can keep this GPA and reach Cum Laude, I could use that for my resume and get a better job.

I do not want to jump off the balcony and into the pool, but my friends would call me a chicken if I don't. (Kids these days).

If I do well on this presentation, my boss will probably give me that promotion I wanted.

I am just going to give this child the toy so they will shut up.

Physiological and dependent focus asks the question *what's in it for me*. Emotional and codependent focus asks the question *how to get this for me*. Your actions may now be for others, but they are so you can have the results you desire. You are now acting, but in anticipation of a specific reaction.

Interdependence

The need to connect the dots and make sense of how everything not only works, but works together, is that of interdependence.

Once a child is around the preschool age, they begin to ask one question: Why? They are constantly trying to understand things and their curiosity at this time is the catalyst for their development. This, in addition to creativity, is what forms endless possibilities, thus leading to the statement "you can be anything you want to be."

The zeal for knowledge and the aspiration for innovation is in direct correlation to spiritual needs (morality, creativity, problem solving, spontaneity, lack of prejudice, and acceptance of facts).

The need to connect the dots and make sense of how everything not only works, but works together, is that of interdependence. Someone that thinks interdependently typically has this voice.

> *I wonder how I can make an impact in this company.*

> *I have been working hard and lost a few hours of sleep, but it is important that I do my best in this project so we can do our best as an organization.*

> *It may not be the easiest thing to do, but it is definitely the right thing to do and that is all that matters.*

> *I know she yelled at me, but I did not yell back because I love her. I do not yell at the people I love, no matter what they may say or do. Her actions do not define mine.*

> *I am going to do my best in this class because I told myself that I will always give 100 percent in the things I am a part of.*

Dependent and physiological needs ask the question *what's in it for me*. Codependence and emotional needs wonder *what can I do to get this for me*. Interdependence and spiritual needs asks *what can I do to better "we."* This proactive thinking feeds off of the character you have developed within. It is constantly discovering how things are related and recognizing that you have a choice in everything.

In order to discover this part of your being, you must dig deep inside and bring out all that you can find.

Proactive Thinking

The fault in thinking physiologically is its importance of instant gratification and not looking far enough in the future to really help you amount to anything.

Ironically, the kiddie pool meant for infants is just too shallow. The fault in thinking physiologically is its importance of instant gratification. Each instance does not look far enough in the future to really help you amount to anything. It is consistently looking in the now and has a very scoped vision of life.

If all she thought about was her divorce the death of a family member, and being homeless as she cared for her baby girl, J.K. Rowling would probably not have been able to write the Harry Potter series.

If all he thought about was how he could benefit from his position and role in the companies he invested in, Warren Buffet would not be one of the richest people in the world.

If all he thought about was being homeless and not having the opportunities to share his talent to the world, Steve Harvey (and A TON of other successful people in the world) would probably be in the same position he was desperately trying to get out of.

When you look at these lives and the lives of many others, you see that they had and continue to have patience and clarity on their long-term goals. You can also see that when growth trumps all, you are capable of doing more than you could ever imagine.

Imagine that I told you that I would give you a hundred dollars if you were capable of getting to a destination fifteen miles away in an hour. If you are in any vehicle, what you have to do seems pretty easy. As long as you do not have to deal with any form of traffic or mechanical malfunction, getting to your destination is nothing but a walk in the park.

Now let's say that *what* you have to do stays the same, but *how* you are to do it changes. You now have to get to this place by foot. This changes the game in its entirety. What was once an easy task is now almost an impossible one (unless you are some skilled, gazelle-running type marathon athlete). (To put this in perspective, the world record for a half-marathon (13.1 miles) is fifty-eight minutes and twenty-three seconds). I know if someone waltzed up to me saying I had to run fifteen miles in an hour, I would literally laugh in their face and tell them that they are crazy because there is no possible way to do it.

Although there is a possible money prize, most of us still would not make the attempt because the task is so much bigger than we think we can do so there is no point of even trying. The reward, although nice, is too shallow (kiddie pool). I mean let's be honest with ourselves; the reward of material things only goes so far for even the most money-hungry individuals.

With that being said, what if I told you to get to a place fifteen miles away in an hour, on foot, in order to save the most important person in your life from being killed. All of a sudden *what* you have to do and *how* you have to do it is irrelevant. The only thing you are worried about is the *why*. Those fifteen miles might as well be fifteen feet because you will doing everything in your power to assure the safety of your father, your wife, your best friend, etc.

*Your purpose is your goal and the **why** of the equation.*

This is the power of deep reasoning, the revelation of the bottom line, and the power of understanding the purpose of a scenario. It is almost comical to recollect how often we neglect to ask the question why when it is obviously the most significant point of understanding. The journey to discover the why uncovers the purpose and releases the power of deep reasoning in any and every circumstance. This is what leads to our victory over any problem.

Your purpose is your goal and the why of the equation. Although the formula could function quite well in a form of inspiration (the money), being *desperate* has more impact than a bunch of housewives on ABC.

The journey to discover the deep reasoning or purpose of any and every circumstance is what leads to its victory.

I heard Eric Thomas use this story about having your purpose being in a form of desperation (paraphrased):

There was a young man who wanted to make a lot of money, so he went to a financial guru and said that he wanted to reach the same level the guru had attained.

So the guru told him, "If you want to be at the same level that I am then I will meet you tomorrow at the beach at 4 a.m."

"The beach?" the young man questioned, "I want to make money, I don't want to swim."

The guru smiled and replied, "If you want to make money then I will meet you tomorrow."

So the young man got to the beach at 4 a.m. in his swimsuit ready to go.

The guru asked the young man, "How bad do you want to be successful?"

"Real bad," the young man replied.

"Then walk out into the water," said the guru.

The young man, despite his thoughts, walked into the water waist deep. The guru, seeing the question marks inside his head, told the young man to walk out a little further.

"Why am I out here?" the young man pondered, "I don't want to be a lifeguard, I want to make money!"

But despite his thoughts, he got to the point that his head was just above water. The guru, still witnessing the doubts of the young man, told him to walk out a little further.

"This is crazy. This man is crazy. He may know how to be successful, but he is crazy," the young man thought, but despite his thoughts, got to the point that his nose was just above the water.

"I thought you wanted to be successful?" the guru asked the young man.

"I do!" the young man yelled.

As soon as he said that, the guru approached him and dunked the head of the young man under the water. As the young man tried to fight off the grasp of the guru, his body began to weaken. Just before he passed out, the guru let the young man surface to finally get air.

As the young man tried to catch his breath, the guru asked him, "When you were under water, what did you want to do?"

The young man replied in between his gasps, "I wanted to breathe."

The guru smiled and told the young man, "When you want to succeed as bad as you wanted to breathe, then you will be successful."

When you are in a position like that, the only thing you can think about is oxygen. You do not care how you get it or what you have to do to get it as long as you can *breathe*. Your purpose should have that same level of commitment in your life. Your purpose needs to be on your mind 24/7 and everything you do should be in relation to it.

Now do not get me wrong, I am not saying that you cannot enjoy recreational moments or take time to relax. If you don't then you will burn out fast. However, working on your purpose needs to be as *natural* as your need to breathe. You do not think about breathing when you are just living your life. Your body naturally knows when to inhale and exhale. Your body, due to its desperate need for oxygen, is constantly *inspired* to let it in.

Most of my writing ideas do not come to me when I am sitting in front of a white computer screen continuously. My thoughts come from being out in the world and hearing someone say something like the kiddie pool analogy, watching some movie, or being in nature and meditating on how amazing life is.

My desperation stimulates my body to discover my inspiration. I do not have to consciously think about my purpose because my subconscious instinctively does it because it is embedded within me. Desperation always renders inspiration, but it is rare for it to go the other way.

Why don't you just go for the latter? If you go for the one, you will get the other. So how do you get to a place of desperation? How do you find what constantly propels you towards your purpose? More importantly, *why* should you get to a place of desperation and learn what your purpose is in life? Why is it so many people do not even try? We will answer these questions in the next chapter, but take a moment and review what you learned in this one.

Key Points

- The fault in thinking physiologically is its importance of instant gratification and not looking far enough in the future to really help you amount to anything.
- When you focus on the physiological, you become dependent on what happens to you and become a victim to everyone and everything around you.
- When you are re-active, not pro-active then whenever life challenges you, you succumb to its hands of power and control by allowing it to be the basis of your actions.
- When you are focused not only on your needs but the way others perceive those needs, you are now in a stage of codependence.
- The need to connect the dots and make sense of how everything not only works, but works together, is that of interdependence.
- Your purpose is your goal and the why of the equation.
- The journey to discover the deep reasoning or purpose of any and every circumstance is what leads to its victory.

Digging Deeper

My stinkin' thinkin' kept me away from moving forward toward my purpose. Read the descriptions below and check off the one best describes where you are right now.

- Dependent and physiological asks *what's in it for me*.
- Codependence and emotional asks *what can I do to get this for me*.

- Interdependence and spiritual asks *what can I do to better for "we."*

Desperation can prompt inspiration as it opens us up to greater possibilities.

So, when desperate, expect inspiration to fill the void the desperation created.

See if you can answers these questions:

How do I get to a place of desperation?

How do I find what constantly propels me towards my purpose?

More importantly, why should I get to a place of desperation and learn what my purpose is in life?

If you could not answer them all, then I suggest you proceed on to the next chapter.

Chapter 3

Why do People Fail to Discover Their Purpose?

A lot of people in society fail to discover their purpose for multiple reasons, but there are two big umbrellas that junction the others.

We Make No Effort

What we know, no matter how painful it may be, can seem better than change sometimes. We grow numb to the pain and begin to believe that it is the best place for us. Anything outside of what we already know leaves us petrified in fear, making it impossible to grow. This frozen status is due to one of the following reasons.

We are too comfortable: There is usually some desperate notion that triggers your need for a purpose. When you are living a "successful" life, at least one that society would deem successful, you believe the advertisement. I know because I was one of them. My life story does not involve any impoverished scenario or unloving home. My father, being a medical doctor, made my life pretty simple. I never lacked anything financially and did not have to worry about making ends meet. As grateful as I am for this, it crippled my desperation beacon. Due to the

Why do People Fail to Discover Their Purpose?

fact that I never had to fight for anything, I did not understand the concept. All I understood was living a nice, comfortable life.

When your life is comfortable due to what you have on the outside, you are miserable because you have nothing on the inside. Each day crushes the person within because you know that there is something more to life than going through the motions. The idea of changing anything, especially into something that could lead into the slightest bit of discomfort, is frightening. In order to avoid this, we come up with any and every reason to not go after a more meaningful life.

When your life is comfortable due to what you have on the outside, you are miserable because you have nothing on the inside.

We look without, as opposed to within. Focusing on the things we lack comes from media and stereotypes brainwashing us into believing that there are specific types of people that do specific types of things. "Race and gender are great for statistics, but terrible excuses," is the way Jonathan Sprinkles puts it. Using your current position as a scapegoat for not reaching your future one is *very* dangerous and deadly. These moments are the moments where you must make a shift mentally and switch the question from *why* to *why not?*

We are too afraid and too insecure. Fear is derived from either not knowing or not fully comprehending someone or something. The information received does not give you enough faith in the object, leading to the misperception of what it is. *Monsters, Inc.* is a prime example of this. (Don't judge the big kid inside of me). In that movie, the little girl, Boo, was afraid of the monster that scared her at night. It was not until she decided to no longer be scared and be proactive that she took her strength back.

The greatness within you is kept buried under the social norms and stereotypical propaganda that you have been taught your entire life.

A lot of students are afraid of calculus (or anything that involves math really) because it is something they do not know. The fear also comes from those that have gone before them and expressed how terrible it was. This leads to the misconceived notion that it is *extremely hard*. When I was picking classes for high school one year, I had the option of taking calculus.

When I addressed the issue with my father, the first thing I said was, "I don't think I can take that class because it will be too hard."

My father just looked at me and said, "Just because it was hard for someone else does not mean that it will be hard for you. Don't let someone else's experience ruin your opportunity."

As a high school student, I was super mad that my dad said that because I knew how right he was. Because I did not fully know what the course was, I relied on the experience of others to make my decision. This is one of the many ways people become insecure in their decision making. Insecurity is the epitome of *not* digging deep due to its collection of comparisons and analytical ridiculousness.

Tests are meant to evaluate where you are in your walk.

The greatness within you is kept buried under the social norms and stereotypical propaganda that you have been taught your entire life, all of which is as far from the truth as fear itself. Examinations and statistical studies have made an implication in the human mind that we have to consistently judge our performance based on the performance of others. It has even boiled down to us judging if we should try to perform something by first referencing the actions of others.

What we have missed is the fact that all of these things were designed for *us* as tests. Tests are meant to evaluate where we are in our walk. They are there to critique *our* retention and preparation so we can take up the results thereafter and adjust accordingly so *we* can do better in *our* future. Fear and insecurity are things that need to be kicked to the side when we are on our way to discover and go after our purpose. They not only do more harm than good, but they are also bold-faced lies that we tell ourselves so we can continue to live in our comfort zone.

Fear and insecurity are things that need to be kicked to the side when we are on our way to discover and go after our purpose.

We Make the Wrong Effort

We live in a time that is not only fast-paced, but very demanding as well. Due to this lifestyle, we miss the importance of a purpose-driven life because what happens in the here and now is what drives us. We make the wrong efforts when we do that. Here are a few reasons why we make the wrong efforts.

We look for fortune and power as opposed to character and relationships. Everywhere you turn, there is another way to make an extra buck and steps to manipulate those around you. As negative as that may sound, that is the bottom line of a lot of things today because we are constantly looking for the easy route. The idea is to do things fast and to make it easy, but that is the complete opposite of a life that goes after purpose. Fortune and power techniques are one-trick ponies that never last. These make-shift recipes create lives that eventually bring us back to ground zero. More often than not, they force us to start all over again with nothing.

On the contrary, character creates a foundation because it lives inside of you. Character is something that you can implement in anything you get your hands on because it is the funnel that you use to consider all of your choices and actions instead of having someone else tell you what to do. In doing so, you create the foundation for strong relationships with people and release the tools that will help you build upward.

Character is something that you can implement in anything you get your hands on.

We look for a living as opposed to living purposefully. Finding a career is what we are all told to do. Since we were kids, we have been asked, "What do you want to be?" and as we get older it goes to "what do you do for a living?" When we are defined by what we do, we pigeon-hole ourselves. Our title limits our options and the impact we are designed to have in this world dwindles down to just a handful. Living purposefully leads to everything having a meaning because it is not about what we do, but who we are. The opportunities we have are never outside our expertise because the mission coincides with it. It does not matter if we change careers or move across the world or even walk your girlfriend's dog because there is a purpose for all of it. Why you do it trumps what you are doing.

Living purposefully leads to everything having a meaning because it is not about what we do, but who we are.

We look for things to be easier as opposed to us becoming better. Jim Rohn used to say, "dont wish it were easier, wish you were better." Are we finding ourselves reading more books and getting more material to figure out a way to make things easier instead of making us better? The greatest part about purpose is the journey itself, not the destination. The lessons we learn from every trial is what prepares us for the next one. The reason we are stuck in the same place and going through the same rut a lot of times is because we are putting Band-Aids on things that are cancerous. We are never getting to the root of the problem.

Your life will not change until you do. Whoever told the world that things are supposed to be easier needs to be revived, shot, and revived again to be shot one more time. There is a reason why they are called growing pains. It is going to be uncomfortable. It is going to challenge you. It is going to give you nights of tears and moments where you will have to break a sweat, but the outcome of all of that is priceless as you become better and dig deeper.

The lessons we learn from every trial is what prepares us for the next one.

Discovering Your Purpose

Production is the only thing on people's minds these days. "The what" and "the how" are at the forefront of our thoughts, and (if we would admit it) the reason why so many things in this world are broken. Students focus on producing good grades so much that they forget that education is for learning and comprehension, not just a letter/number grade. Employees focus on producing just enough to keep the monkey off their back and forget that there is a reason why they have that position. Mom and dad focus so much on providing for their family that they ignore the most important aspect: the family!

Understanding the why, the purpose, puts you in a better position for success because its understanding is what leads to your production.

One of the greatest moments in someone's life is discovering their purpose. When you discover your purpose, you discover why you are here. Each day your bottom line ascends to another level as you grow outside of yourself. Every action made towards your purpose is more superior to any needs you may have and desires of personal gain. All in all, it gives you a better understanding of *who you are*.

If it is most important for us to work from the end and not wait until the end, then we must travel forward in time to discover what it is we are really pursuing in life.

The End Game

It is a warm, autumn day. The numerous colors around you representing the resolution of life and flourishing times is a great parallel for this very moment. At a very mature age, you sit surrounded by family and friends celebrating the time that has passed thus far. Being around nature as the band plays your favorite tunes brings you to a place of serenity and peace as your past and present collide into this stream of constancy that never really goes away.

One by one, people step up to the stage to talk about you and your *greatness*. What are they saying about you? What have you accomplished? Which key words are being used to describe your character? How do these individuals explain your importance to them? Which moments do they vividly remember? These questions (among others) will be necessary as you search for your purpose.

As we take this journey, you will learn what really matters to you most. You will find out who you are inside. You will understand what you may have been missing up until this point because you lacked your purpose. For those who have discovered theirs, this will be an opportunity to dig deeper into it.

I am literally trying to control my emotions as I write this because this is such a transitional time in your life (as it was for mine). The fact that you have chosen to let me grow in my purpose by allowing this book to help you discover yours is truly an honor. It is going to be a rigorous, and even scary task at times. You will laugh. You will cry. The good, the bad, and the ugly may be put to light, but do not be discouraged. All aspects of your life need to be understood so you can discover *the* aspect of your life.

The Circles of Purpose

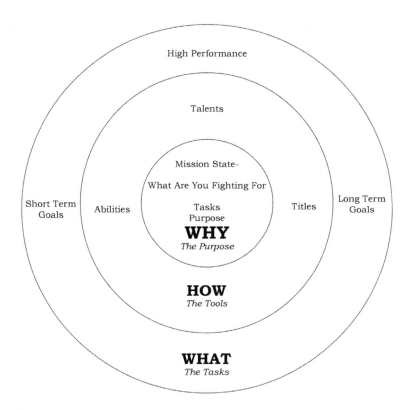

In order to discover your purpose, you must do some pretty intense research on the one thing many of us avoid: *yourself*. This will be the only time that someone will actually allow you to be the center of the universe (literally and figuratively) as we unravel the future that has been predestined for your success.

When I say "all the answers are within you" I am not saying "you have all the answers." Understanding your purpose goes outside you as a person because it goes into what I consider your *spiritual being*. Not to sound too ethereal or sci-fi, but there is something that connects all of us. Hollywood, religion, science and everything in between agrees that someone (or something) created all of us and lives inside of us as an intercessor for our connectivity.

We all have come to the conclusion that our life is not just happenstance and our actions have meaning. Our connection to one another is the key to all things. Discovering that part within yourself is what creates the paradigm that gives you all the answers and brings you to the reality that what you do, at any given moment, is the only thing that separates you from past and future. In essence, the reason why all the answers are within you is due to all the answers are coinciding within *us*.

It is in this mind shift, in conjunction to "you" being a sacrifice for the "we", that you are able to connect to all things that had, have and will come. It is in this thought process that the discoveries, actions, understandings, and knowledge given to you is designed for the sake of all because all that has happened to you directly and indirectly has lead you to such things.

Call it as you may, this is what takes you through the circles of purpose. It is what binds all three together and assures its success. The circles of purpose are based on the same three questions that have been the resounding motive for discovering your purpose thus far: What, how, and why.

The What is the task(s) that one must accomplish to achieve the overall goal. In military jargon, these are the skirmishes and battles within the war. These goals can take a couple hours or a couple decades to accomplish depending on what they are; but they should be in relation to the theme that is given in the why.

The How are the tools you will use to accomplish the tasks within the small (and eventually big) picture. Just like the fifteen-mile destination analogy, this gives you a wide range of possibilities. For our purposes, these devices are specific to you and you alone as we pay attention to your talents, abilities, and titles.

The Why reveals the main theme of your purpose. This is the one thing that will always be a constant. If everything else falls into unfortunate ruin, this strong foundation remains to rebuild upon.

Each circle has its importance and will help you dig deep and find that person that you want to be. The person that you will be is three in one, as it encompasses your past, present, and future simultaneously in a form of unanimity within your inner being that connects to the universe. The entire conundrum is a question within a question that clears out all the junk that is covering up the better you. It sounds very Yoda-esque, but it is quite simple once you dive into it. We will begin with the inner-most circle of why in the next chapter, young Padawan.

Key Points

- When your life is comfortable due to what you have on the outside, you are miserable because you have nothing on the inside.
- The greatness within you is kept buried under the social norms and stereotypical propaganda that you have been taught your entire life.
- Tests are meant to evaluate where you are in your walk.
- Fear and insecurity are things that need to be kicked to the side when you are on your way to discover and go after your purpose.
- Character is something that you can implement in anything you get your hands on.
- Living purposefully leads to everything having a meaning because it is not about what you do, but who you are.
- The lessons you learn from every trial is what prepares you for the next one.
- Understanding the why, the purpose, puts you in a better position for success because its understanding is what leads to your production.

Digging Deeper

We Make No Effort - check off the excuses that apply to your life right now.

- I am too comfortable.

- I look without, as opposed to within.
- I am too afraid and too insecure.

We Make the Wrong Effort – Check off any that apply to your life right now.

- I look for fortune and power as opposed to character and relationships.
- I look for a living as opposed to living purposefully.
- I look for things to be easier as opposed to becoming better.

Are you ready to discover the why, the purpose, so you can be in a better position for success?

In order to discover your purpose, you must do some pretty intense research on the one thing many of us avoid, *ourselves*. Are you ready to continue?

Chapter 4

The Why

*We learn how to fix things, but never how to **prevent** them from breaking.*

Teachings today focus on solving problems and overcoming obstacles. Although these teachings are not necessarily incorrect, they are incomplete. Our education gives us the solutions, but never the knowledge necessary to create on our own. This leads us to be in a dependent position. We learn how to fix things, but never how to *prevent* them from breaking.

Imagine you went to the doctor's office because you are having pains in your knee. The doctor takes an X-ray, asks you a few questions, and finally just gives you a prescription to relieve the pain. Problem "solved." When you have knee pain, you just pop the pill. Now I do not know about you, but the last thing I want to do is be dependent on a pill to relieve my pain, especially when you risk your body adapting to tolerability and possible addiction because of it! The medication may be taking care of the pain, but not the *source* of the pain.

Let's rewind the tape and head back to the doctor's office. This time around he talks about a few exercises and stretches that you can do to help strengthen your knee and prevent the pain from coming back. Then he talks about natural herbs that can be used as an alternative to the prescription if you would prefer that. He suggests a few things you could change in your diet to assist recovery and sustain your joints. *Then*, he gives you a brace that you can wear for a couple weeks as you recover, along with a program so the brace is more of a tool when you are active or having an episode. You now leave the office with something to *fix* the current problem, as well as ways to *prevent* it in the future, not to mention a number of options.

If you would not want to leave your doctor's office without having a prevention plan, then why do you let it happen in your life, career, relationships, etc.? Tools and steps fix the problem, but virtues and principles prevent the problem and that is what we will be focus on when discovering "the why" of your purpose.

Tools and steps fix the problem, but virtues and principles prevent the problem.

The Big Picture

When I first started to realize the importance of virtues and principles, I was in conversation with a possible client that ran a local church. As we sat and discussed what it is that he was requesting of me, I began to ask the stereotypical consulting questions:

"What is your mission statement?"

"How does the organization operate?"

"What does the chain of command look like?"

"What are the three most important things a person should get out of being a member of your church?"

The more questions I asked, the more he was giving me that confused look on his face because the man did not have the answers to *any* of these questions.

I finally asked, "Do you at least have a church manual or a written-set of policies and procedures for the different ministries and the church as a whole?"

This lead to the expected response, "Well why do you think I am talking to you?"

The Why

I cannot fathom how an organization could function without something so vital. "The pot calling the kettle black," I thought when I realized that I did not have anything like that for myself!

The first thing I did when I returned to my office was actually write out a mission statement, talk about how I wanted to run my life, rank what was most important to me, and how to protect all of it from any personal actions of carnage by implementing consequential procedures and a supportive group for checks and balances.

When you really think about it, our personal lives are a business. We have cash flow. We may not acknowledge it, but we have mission statements and a plan of operations. We have customers, colleagues, and superiors. We have goals and plans for the future with deadlines and evaluations. We have a product (ourselves) and it is necessary for that product to be marketed correctly in order to successfully achieve our purpose. Yet we still like to fly by the seat of our pants and avoid putting in a proper structure to keep our lives organized. It is to no surprise that so many of us struggle daily. Luckily for us, the way we solve the problem and assure its prevention is by defining and acting out our purpose.

The first step in defining your purpose is discovering your big picture. Referring back to the garden party, think about those key words you want people to say about you at that ripe age. Take a moment and write down three to five words that you want to be the theme of your life from now until its natural end.

- *What do these words mean to you?*
- *What must you do daily so others can verify your character?*
- *Why are these specific virtues so important to you?*
- *What happened in your life or who has influenced you in your life that inspired you to become these three to five words?*

Foundation of Purpose

Architects always think functionality before glamour when they are creating a structure. Without a proper understanding of the purpose of the building, it is impossible for them to meet the needs of their client. The one thing that any person that is in the world of construction will tell you is that the foundation of a building is the most important. Without it, you cannot build up or out. If it is faulty, it can lead to the collapse of the structure and bringing everything back to ground zero. There is a specific order that they go through to build a foundation. As we go through the order, we are going to put on our hard hats and build the foundation of our purpose.

These are the steps necessary to do so:

- Dig a deep hole for the foundation
- Set footings to spread the weight of the foundation and keep the foundation aligned
- Make the concrete for your foundation
- Pour the concrete into the form in a constant flow for your foundation
- Let the concrete dry for your foundation
- Remove the form for your foundation
- Keep the concrete wet for a few days to sustain the foundation

These steps, when we look at it in the parallel universe of building the foundation of our purpose, looks like this:

- Depth: *The spirit of your foundation*

There has to be more to your purpose than personal gain. Having that kiddie pool mentality will only get you so far. Those that are successful today always state that the first (and sometimes the second) time they failed was because they did not have enough

The Why

depth in character which, in part, leads to a lack of depth in purpose. Your goals should have a mentality that reaps benefits for you *and* others. Jumping straight to the spiritual portion of our hierarchy is what guarantees your success, the success of others, and takes care of the physical and emotional needs that we have.

We have already spoken of the different names that are used in our society to explicate this phenomena and it is the incalculable piece that every person and organization acknowledges to be the most beneficial factor to the equation of success. In *Strategy Maps*, Robert G. Kaplan and David P. Norton say, "Intangible assets-those not measured by a company's financial system-account for more than 75 percent of a company's value. The average company's tangible assets-the net book value of assets less liabilities-represent less than 25 percent of market value."

What is true for companies is even truer for countries. Some countries, such as Venezuela and Saudi Arabia, have high physical resource endowments but have made poor investments in their people and systems. As a consequence, they produce far less output per person, and experience much slower growth rates than countries such as Singapore and Taiwan that have few natural resources but invest heavily in human and informational capital and effective internal systems. At both the macroeconomic and microeconomic levels, intangible assets drive long-term value creation.

A book, published by Harvard Business School Press (as in *thee* Harvard B-School Press), openly admits that the intelligence and heart of an individual exceeds the value of most and all things we would consider to be important to even grow countries, but we still choose to act as if the spirit within you and me is some hippie image created to bring "unity and tranquility to all (as I raise the peace sign, to the sky)." The results do bring those things (and much more), but the interdependence between us all is very real and it is found by us creating the depth in our souls for our foundation, which is our purpose.

"You don't have a [spirit], you are a [spirit]. You have a body," states C.S. Lewis.

- Footings/Barriers: *The focus of your foundation*

An issue that many of us can come across not only when we build our purpose, but even as we excel in it thereafter, is losing focus. There are moments when we try to do more than we can handle at the time. Other times we may be way on the other side of the fence and go outside the boundaries of our purpose. This happens to most of us because we either have no purpose or because our purpose has yet to solidify. Everything that crosses our mind as interesting is suddenly our new point of attraction, which keeps us floating out in the land of dreams and aspirations. Goals and plans help us be grounded, but they do not keep us grounded. Goals and plans can only be defined by first defining your purpose. Here again, we are looking at the what(s) as oppose to the *why*. Focus is a long-lasting battle that demands our attention at all times in order to uphold our desires. Once we exceed our potential and get to the position we have sought after, then it is time to let our focus shift onto bigger and better things.

Goals and plans can only be defined by first defining your purpose.

- Making the Concrete: *The effort of your foundation (the what)*

Once we have deeply embedded our purpose into our spirits and the intangible, and allowed ourselves to scope it into a more focused and possible place for organization, we will go from the why of our foundation to the what. If you ever had to fix your driveway or secure a fence post, you learned how difficult it is to make concrete. The effort required to make a big bowl of random particles and water into matter that can uphold weight by the tons takes a lot of energy and time. Your foundation, after formulated in the mind, must be generated all over again in this dimension. This is how it shifts from dream to reality.

- Pouring the concrete: ***The fluidity and consistency of your foundation (the how)***

Smooth and controlled flow inspires evenness and stability for your purpose. Its success comes from the avenues that have and will be formed in your life by the titles that are a part of you. Talents and abilities also play a huge role in this aspect with all opportunities being dependent on who you are as a person. As long as you stay in your lane and continue to let what is natural flow and be consistent, how you go about your purpose will always be successful.

- Letting the concrete dry: ***The impact of your foundation***

There will come a time when each of us must evaluate what has happened to better plan for what will happen in the days to come. This moment to pause and ponder what comes next is not there to be idle because your purpose is already in full motion. It is there for you to see if you are heading in the right direction. So many of us want to just keep on pushing forward with our heads down that when we look up we are nowhere near where we desire to be. When the concrete dries, it takes a lot more effort to break it up and start all over again. It is vital to keep everything in a singular motion and to gauge its impact before taking the next step.

- Removing the forms/barriers: ***The expansion of your foundation***

After the foundation has officially been made and is up and running, the time to challenge its formality is underway. How far and how high your structure goes depends on how strong your purpose is inside you. When you can no longer work on your purpose by yourself or with the few you have alongside you, there is a problem, but a good problem. Expansion is a pure sign of growth because the main focus for us is to exceed our potential, not just meet it. The time you and/or your crew outdo yourselves is the time to recognize the success that has come and the success that is to come. It could be children and/or marriage for a couple, the building of a new firm or product for an organization, or writing a book. Each of these relate to the expansion of your horizon and influence as you continue to grow in your purpose and exceed your potential.

Expansion is a pure sign of growth because the main focus for us is to exceed our potential, not just meet it.

- Wetting the concrete: *The sustenance of your foundation*

Many of us may reach our potential, but very few exceed it. The reason is due to our lack of sustenance. The idea is not to sustain the success made, but to sustain its continuation. Wanting to do more and be more is not a negative thing, though wanting it solely for personal gain is. We focus on growing ourselves and our purposes respectively in order to take our world to the next level of understanding and connection. It is natural for us to grow each and every single day.

Trees live decades with the purpose of reaching up to the sky. Families have companies, legacies, and even family names that are designed to live from generation to generation. Thoughts and ideas are recorded and written to live throughout time. Inventions and innovations beget their predecessor to make our future indefinite.

In the movie *Limitless*, the protagonist had the capability to access every memory in his mind. Every book read or lesson heard was recorded and made as easily attainable as looking up a file on your computer. He never tried to sustain the success he made in the movie because he sustained his growing pattern by educating himself at all times and taking new risks that put him outside of his comfort zone. Although our efforts may not be as unparalleled as this man, they can be to the only one that matters: *YOU*!

You beating you every day by taking even the smallest micro step forward makes your future limitless. As long as you remember to keep your purpose meaningful and deep inside your spirit as you take action within your current parameters, then what may be impossible for you today will come to fruition tomorrow.

You beating you every day by taking even the smallest micro step possible to beat the person you were yesterday makes your future limitless.

Going through each of these seven steps will not only build your foundation, but it will make it so solid that it does not matter what you put on top of it because it will be capable of holding up anything. Character building is an art that is discovered after realizing which characteristics are valuable to you. When you have those values be the foundation of your life, anything is possible.

Ñ *Key Points*

- Ñ We learn how to fix things, but never how to *prevent* them from breaking.
- Ñ Tools and steps fix the problem, but virtues and principles prevent the problem.
- Ñ "You don't have a [spirit], you are a [spirit]. You have a body," states C.S. Lewis.
- Ñ Goals and plans can only be defined by first defining your purpose.
- Ñ Expansion is a pure sign of growth because the main focus for us is to exceed our potential, not just meet it.
- Ñ You beating you every day by taking even the smallest micro step possible to beat the person you were yesterday makes your future limitless.

Ñ Character building is an art that is discovered after realizing which characteristics are valuable to you. When you have those values be the foundation of your life, anything is possible.

Digging Deeper

Check these steps off as you work toward discovering your purpose:

p Write out a mission statement,
p Talk about how I want to run my life,
p Rank what is most important to me, and
p Protect all of it from any personal actions of carnage by implementing consequential procedures and a supportive group for checks and balances.

Write down three to five words that you want to be the theme of your life when it comes to its natural end. Then answer these questions.

_____ _____ _____ _____ _____

- *What do these words mean to me?*
- *What must I do daily so others can verify my character?*
- *Why are these specific virtues so important to me?*
- *What happened in my life or who has influenced and inspired me to become these three to five words?*

You beating you every day by taking even the smallest micro step possible to beat the person you were yesterday makes your future limitless.

Journal how you beat you every day starting today.

Character building is an art that is discovered after realizing which characteristics are valuable to you. When you have those values be the foundation of your life, anything is possible.

What did you discover is valuable to you in the foundation of your life?

Chapter 5

L.O.V.E.

Your purpose is something that you more than likely have been doing all this time, but never noticed. Some of us do not have the luxury of having our career and purpose to be one in the same (yet), but outside of work and school, it is something that you strive to accomplish. Your purpose is either about something you love or about something you hate and want the world to be ridden of. Your actions form to combat an evil or to support a positive that is necessary for human development. The L.O.V.E. factor of your purpose is discovered in these categories.

L - Lost (lose track of time thinking about/things done to get away)
O - Open (things that you are always caught in the forefront doing)
V - Value (volunteer/virtues)
E - Expertise (things that people always come to you for help in)

L.O.V.E.

Lost in Something You Love

"If you were lost on an island, what are the five things you would want to have with you?"

We have all heard, if not been asked, this question at some point in our lives. The inquiry is designed to better understand an individual by placing us in a position of desperation and isolation for an allotted time that equates to eternity. But instead of being lost on an island or in a J.J. Abrams television show, let's think about moments when you are lost in your thoughts. It is very easy for us to get lost in our thoughts. The question is not if, but why you get lost in them.

When you get lost in your thoughts intentionally, you need a compass inside you that can get you back to your point of origin.

Sometimes we get lost in our thoughts intentionally because we want to escape from something or get away from someone. Other times we do it for revelation. When you get lost intentionally, you need a compass inside you that can get you back to your point of origin. You are placing bread crumbs along the trail like Hansel and Gretel so you can remember how you got to each thought or idea. In terms of thought processing, this is great because you not only have a way to remember how you got to a point, but you are making it possible to divert onto other paths because you have created a new familiar place.

In jazz music, you do not get a piece of music that tells you what to do note-for-note. Instead, there is a chart that gives you the chord progression or general idea of the song. The musician is given the chance to "get lost" in the music and interpret it whichever way they see fit as long as it is within the parameters of the chord progression. Each chord written is a bread crumb that lets you know where you just were as you explore other ways to get to the next. The more you explore, the more options you will have. That one chord not only has different ways of being played in terms of note order, but how you get from it to another also has a limitless boundary as you look at it from a number perspective, a key perspective, a mode perspective, or even the perspective of a specific instrument or groups of instruments!

When you intentionally get lost, you are looking for new places to reach from the last bread crumb you placed because it goes far and beyond something that you do. The continuation of questions as you dive into unchartered territory happens because it is what you love.

When you intentionally get lost in your thoughts, you are looking for new places to reach from the last bread crumb you placed because it is what you love.

My initial "lost tracks" involved music and driving. At a very early age, I played instruments and enjoyed what tunes do to the soul. As I got older, music literally was my life for quite some time as I traveled the world with a singing group. I am also the type of person that has a playlist for every mood and activity because I listen to any and everything to get to "that place." From work to play, music augments my thoughts and gives me an angle on my tasks. (I was probably listening to music as I wrote this section and many others in this book).

Driving does the same exact thing for me. If you give me a full tank of gas and a day that has nothing on the marquee, finding me will be nearly impossible. You would be lucky to even find me in the same state at times. Hopping on the open road with the top down and the wind pressed against my face gives me a feeling of openness and freedom to explore the world and its endless possibilities. I will randomly turn onto unpaved roads and stop by some diner that I just know will have some good home cooking inside. (I look for the pick-up trucks. Dead giveaway).

Now it is your turn. Start by looking at the things that you may take for granted because you do it all the time. Walk around your house or your room and look for patterns. What do you have a lot of? What don't you have a lot of? Think about what you catch yourself doing when you are in a place of silence or transitioning from one room to the next. Where is your rabbit hole, Alice, and what do you always take with you when you go there? Perhaps you can take a moment and ask a loved one or friend what they see you doing whenever they "sneak up on you."

This second-tier (but definitely not second place) level of lost is one that I have missed for years before someone brought it up to me. Actually, if that person had not pointed it out to me, this book probably would not have been written. I did not realize how much I *loved* writing. The idea of writing always reverted me back to essays and theses during my years in school so it always had a negative connotation. That in turn led it to *not* being one of the things I use to intentionally get lost in. But when I rummaged through my old things, I found a mountain of notebooks that I used to journal. There were endless scraps of paper and cup holsters that I would write a random thought on or use to express my feelings at that given time. It was a world that I have been creating for years and I never even noticed it!

I even had the habit of keeping a pen and pad on me at all times thinking it was a proper thing to do. It never occurred to me that it was a habit because it was my go-to place for escape. As a friend of mine puts it, "You don't know what you don't know." I did *not know* I actually enjoyed writing. Take your time and really think about what you do to escape as well. Begin to try and identify those "lost tracks" you have in your life.

Open to Act on What You Love

Getting lost in the things you love is what you do for yourself on the inside. Being open to the things you love is what you do for others on the outside. These are things that you would do for a fee or for free because your bottom line is you getting out there and doing it. Sometimes you are forced to get out there and do it because you are so open to it and others notice that. A good friend of mine is that way with speaking.

Getting lost in the things you love is what you do for yourself on the inside. Being open to act on the things you love is what you do for others on the outside.

My buddy aspires to have his own television talk show just like the queen of it all, Lady Oprah Winfrey. His desire to go out there and learn about people while inspiring others is a trait he has always had and will continue to have because it is who he is. He is the type of guy who can sit there and listen to your life story for hours and have you feel as if the two of you have been best friends your entire life.

He is a man that can grab a microphone and talk about anything as he engages the audience and challenges them with his words of wisdom. It was no wonder he was asked (without any other option) to talk whenever we represented our university. He was always either next to or across from any dignitary at any meal as the ambassador of our campus. He loved doing it because communicating and understanding people is a part of his purpose.

There is only one thing you want rendered when it involves what you are open to do for your purpose and that is action. Something euphoric is released within when putting what you love into action. While some would be exhausted from the experience, you are trying to find ways to act on it over and over again. It is a high without an exterior component. There is a joy that flutters despite your attitude prior to engaging in the activity. You are caught in the forefront because it is your forefront to have. The floor is yours. Be open and act on what you love and you will most likely be acting on your purpose.

Value

What lesson are you capable of teaching by upholding it in your daily life?

One of the most important things you can use to define your purpose is your character. Character is a word that has lost its mojo somewhere along the way, and for a number of reasons. One's character is built upon the virtues and values that they deem worthwhile, as in valuable. On top of the fact that defining your virtues and values requires a lot of soul searching and time, its "lack of tangibility" in society has made it pointless. We must recognize how important it is and why it is so important to finding and fulfilling our purpose.

If your why is your purpose and it is the foundation of your existence, your character is the foundation of the real you. There are questions that must be answered when you are looking for what you value and the virtues that will define your character.

How do you want people to feel?

How do you want people to feel about you?

If someone was to describe you with one word, what would it be?

What do you want to be the beacon for you in this lifetime and thereafter?

What lesson are you capable of teaching by upholding it in your daily life?

Discovering the answers to these questions will be the foundation necessary to always give you an opportunity to excel in life. This is the secret to the millionaires and billionaires in our world today because most of them have not had the smoothest of rides to the top of the economy. If you look at most of these big wigs in finance, they have often lost a lot before finally "figuring it out." A lot of them have even filed for bankruptcy once or twice, hitting financial rock bottom before reaching their mountaintop. How did they do this? Well, the only way to accomplish such a feat is by having a solid foundation and purpose.

You can only create a solid purpose by solidifying character.

Expertise

Each of us are really good at *something*.

Last, but not least, a great way to help find your purpose at any given moment is by understanding what you are really good at. In knowing your strengths, you are capable of not only discovering your purpose in life, but discovering your purpose in all of its aspects. Each of us are really good at *something*. It does not have to be precise like a doctorate in some field or a specialty in a course. The reality is that those positions were met due to discovering that *something you are really good at*.

In knowing your strengths, you are capable of not only discovering your purpose in life, but discovering your purpose in all of its aspects.

Walt Disney was really good at challenging people, which is why his company grew. Frank Sinatra was really good at communicating and that lead to his successful career in entertainment. Mark Cuban is really good at pinpointing success and that is why he sits on the list of wealthiest people in the world. Olivia Pope is really good at fixing things and that is why she has her own dramatized television series that everyone (and their momma) watches religiously.

Their success did not come because they were great artists, singers, entrepreneurs, or lawyers. Those were just the outlets each chose to live within their purpose. Go back in your mind to figure out the one thing that you are not only open with in terms of acting on it, but open with by squeezing it into different fields and occupations as well.

Key Points

- When you get lost in your thoughts intentionally, you need a compass inside you that can get you back to your point of origin.
- When you intentionally get lost in your thoughts, you are looking for new places to reach from the last bread crumb you placed because it is what you love.
- Getting lost in the things you love is what you do for yourself on the inside. Being open to act on the things you love is what you do for others on the outside.
- Each of us are really good at *something*.
- You can only create a solid purpose by building your character.
- In knowing your strengths, you are capable of not only discovering your purpose in life, but discovering your purpose in all of its aspects.

Digging Deeper

Take your time and really think about what you do to escape.

During these times when you are lost in your thoughts, what do you catch yourself doing?

Which path do you take to bring you to back to a position of control?

Ask a loved one or friend what they see you doing whenever they "sneak up on you."

Write down anything that comes to mind. Editing things before you put it on paper is the number one no-no (with the stern finger and flapping of the wrist). Let your thoughts flow from your mind and through the pen that separates it from being a moment and lasting forever.

Be open to act on what you love. Act on your purpose.

What would you do today if there was nothing on the marquee and no limit on your time?

You can only create a solid purpose by building your character.

How do you want people to feel?

How do you want people to feel about you?

If someone was to describe you with one word, what would it be?

What do you want to be the beacon for you in this lifetime and thereafter?

What lesson are you capable of teaching by upholding it in your daily life?

Go back in your mind to figure out the one thing that you are not only open with in terms of acting on it, but open with by squeezing it into different fields and occupations as well.
What is it?

Chapter 6

Creating Your Purpose Statement

Now that we have all the pieces to the puzzle for your *why*, it is time to put your purpose into writing. This general overview of who you are and who you are striving to be is the first part of digging deep within yourself and will help you define your actions. This is a very simplified version of your purpose statement, but you can go into further detail hereafter. These points will have the capability of changing throughout your lifetime as you grow. Your purpose statement is essentially your thesis for this book called life so if you change it then you will have to change the book in its entirety. If you think about it in terms of building a foundation, it takes a lot more effort to destroy what you already built than just taking your time to really figure out what it is you want to share with the world.

The equation for this purpose statement is: I, [insert name here], will represent [insert values] by [lost discovery], [open discovery], and [expertise discovery].

This is your purpose for living and the reason *why* you have been placed here at this given time. Now it is time to figure out *how* you will accomplish it.

The How

After discovering *why* your purpose is important and meaningful, you must figure out *how* you will bring it to fulfillment. If the *why* is the reason, then the *how* are the tools used to make your reason a reality. The tools used to make your purpose a reality are opportunities to excel within it. Talents and skills are used as tools to make your *why* happen. The best way to understand this is to imagine you are in an empty classroom without a person in sight. In the distance, there is a whiteboard.

As you get closer to the whiteboard, you realize that something is written on it. It is your name. Underneath your name there is a caption that asks: "What are your titles?" This is what will allow you to see what your *how* options are. Any talent, family relation, skill, job title, relationship status, and hobby that you use to describe yourself from when you were born up until now should be put up on that board. In essence, you are brainstorming and writing everything that you can remember about yourself.

Each element on your whiteboard is a venue that can be used to implement your purpose. Each *how* is a place to act on your *why*. For instance, if you are/were a football player, you can use football to fill in [insert values]. You can signify [insert values] with your family because you are a sister and a mother. Each "title" is just another way for you to put your character and purpose into the world. This is how we make the big picture, smaller and more comprehensive.

What was once perceived as some whimsical dream can now be a tangible possibility, but it does not stop there. As much as you are doing good for this world that we are all a part of, you are also doing yourself good as you "practice what you preach." Now the person you want to be is being worked on constantly because you are seeing how the big picture can be put into little moments. In doing so, those "little" moments will not be so little anymore as you impact your life and the lives of others. Mind you, the more titles you have, the more chances you have to make a difference. There is a wonderful parable about talents in Scripture that illustrates this concept.

"For the kingdom of heaven is like a man traveling to a far country, who called his own servants and delivered his goods to them. And to one he gave five talents, to another two, and to another one, to each according to his own ability; and immediately he went on a journey. Then he who had received the five talents went and traded with them, and made another five talents. And likewise he who had received two gained two more also. But he who had received one went and dug in the ground, and hid his lord's money. After a long time the lord of those servants came and settled accounts with them.

"So he who had received five talents came and brought five other talents, saying, 'Lord, you delivered to me five talents; look, I have gained five more talents besides them.' His lord said to him, 'Well done, good and faithful servant; you were faithful over a few things, I will make you ruler over many things. Enter into the joy of your lord.' He also who had received two talents came and said, 'Lord, you delivered to me two talents; look, I have gained two more talents besides them.' His lord said to him, 'Well done, good and faithful servant; you have been faithful over a few things, I will make you ruler over many things. Enter into the joy of your lord."
(Matthew 25:14-23 NKJV)

How fitting is it to have the currency named talents. To whom much is given, much is required so more may be required of you if you have more talents and skills. It states that you are never given more than you can handle (1 Corinthians 10:13). It may seem that you have been given a liability because you have all of these venues to act on your purpose, but it should be looked as an opportunity as the meaning of your life can be played out time and time again.

The issue is not the number of talents you have to implement your purpose, it is the effort put into those talents that is most important.

When you look at really successful people in our society, they are really successful because they have many opportunities to bring their purpose to life. If you do not have that many lines connecting to your name, you will once you give 100 percent effort in the ones you currently have. Sir Isaac Newton's third law of motion states, "When one body exerts a force on a second body, the second body simultaneously exerts a force equal in magnitude and opposite in direction on the first body."

The issue is not the number of talents you have to implement your purpose, it is the effort put into those talents that is most important. Remember that it is all about exceeding *your* potential. Character is built by behavior and a behavior is formed by habits. Habits are made by repetition using all of your mind, body, and soul. Giving 100 percent effort to accomplishing your tasks is what renders the most **of you** as well as the most **for you**. If you put in the work, you will see the reward. What is 100 percent effort? The only way we can really know is by figuring out the final part of our equation, the *what*.

Goals are dreams with a measurement and deadline.

The What

The bottom line of it all and what calculates our success is the *what*. The *what* is the act itself. It is *what* this variable equates to at the very end of it all as we achieve *what* we shall now and always will consider our goals. A goal is anything that we want to reach by proactively going after it with the tools we have within ourselves in order to make our purpose a reality. A purpose is not some inanimate object of our imagination that is not capable of escaping our minds into our hands; unless we fail to shift it into a goal.

Goals are dreams with a measurement and deadline. A goal is tangible because it can be calculated and understood by someone other than yourself. We do need to acknowledge though, that goals at times have other names that are ugly and cynical. This is not work. It should not be a chore. Our *what* must always be referred to as an opportunity to make our purpose real. If we try to make it anything else, we will make what we love to do into just another J-O-B and that is not the point of this at all. Remember the analogy with the fifteen-mile trail. Money is not the motivation we want to have! It needs to go beyond that and be outside of ourself in order for it to really be something worth while.

Goal setting can be put into these categories:

1. Educational
2. Family
3. Influential
4. Experimental

Having these categories will allow you to reach every aspect of your potential because it covers all of what is necessary to see what you are really made of.

Educational

The concept that knowledge is power is very true as long as the knowledge sinks in and is put into action.

Where do we get the notion that once we get our diploma that learning is over? We have looked at education as some type of bacteria that we must deal with and that its cure is walking into the real world where study and research are designed for brown-nosers and interns. However, the complete opposite is true for those that excel in the world so it must be the opposite for you and me as well.

One thing I love to do when I am lounging around is to look at houses. Architecture has always been something that I thought about getting into. Pictures and videos that give you the tour of these luxurious homes built for the wealthy of this world make you wonder if the gods themselves implanted artistry and glamor into the minds of those that dreamed of these magnificent palaces.

If you enjoy looking at these homes the way I do, have you ever noticed a similarity? There is always one recurring theme in these mansions and that is the fact that there is always a library with *tons* of books! These successful individuals with the expensive cars and multiple homes always have a place to be alone with the knowledge of mankind. The people that lead our society in any and every aspect do not stop their education after shaking the hand of the university representative at the end of the stage. On the contrary, their understanding of the importance of knowledge goes far beyond anything that involves making their houses look pretty and formal. The concept that knowledge is power is very true as long as the knowledge sinks in and is put into action.

In high school, graduation day was called commencement. At that fragile age, I just assumed that commencement was a synonym for graduation. (I know. Stupid). Up until this point in my life, I thought graduation day was a celebration of what has ended when it is supposed to be a springboard into what the future holds. Commencement means *beginning*. Graduation is what propels you into the intelligence discovered in life by *your* hands. No more teachers and assignments required, but there is still a requirement to grow mentally in order to take your life to its next place. Educational goals can range from reading one book a month to taking a course at your local university in your field or even learning a new language. The education you desire should match the track you are currently on so it can match the track your purpose is on.

Family

Between the number of unhappiness and divorces, parents trying to keep up with the financial squeeze of society, and the distractions that media has implemented for our children, the concept of family is deteriorating at a rapid pace. However, we need family as a part of our purpose statement because they play a very huge role in our lives. The unfortunate part to it all is we can become so focused on reaching our goals and meeting their needs that we forget to appreciate those we are fighting so hard for.

When I was barely in grammar school, both my parents worked at a hospital. My father ran his own practice and my mother assisted him in all that he did. My grandmother raised me and my little sister throughout most of it, but I vividly remember how often I wanted to take my father's beeper and throw it in the trash. The house we lived in and the clothes we wore could never meet the desire I had to spend time with my mom and dad. As I got older, my parents did have more time to spare at home, but it was too late by then as I transitioned to boarding school and college. Now do not get the wrong idea. I love my parents and my parents love me (in spite of the fact that they shipped me off. . .twice). I enjoyed my childhood. I would not change a thing about my past because it is what happened then that makes me who I am now. But (and this is a *big* but), I know that I would have chosen one more vacation, movie night, or even one of my sister's choir recitals (as lame as they might have been) over enough funds for unnecessary Christmas gifts or the bigger television in the family room.

It is important to not only excel in your purpose and potential, but to appreciate it with the ones around you.

There is a story about a little boy coming to his father one day after a long day at work.

The little boy asked his dad, "How much money do you make?"

"I am not sure son. Enough to keep this family afloat," the dad replied.

"Well how much do you make an hour?" he questioned his father.

"I don't know son. Let's just say $40 an hour. Why are you asking me this?" he responded tiredly because the only thing he was thinking about was sleep.

The little boy left his father for a moment and went into his room. After rummaging through his things, he finally returned with his piggy bank and said, "I know this is not $40 daddy, but can I give you this so we can play for an hour?"

The father wept in shock at this revelation. All this time he was working hard for his family, but he forgot to spend time with them.

He picked up his son and told him, "You do not have to pay me a dime. Let's go in your room and do whatever you want to do."

The reason family is a part of our what *is because many of us will forget to enjoy the people we love the most if we do not include them in our goals.*

Whether it is with each person in your family individually or the compilation of them all, it is important to set long-term goals to check off the bucket list for the family that you have now and the family you will have in the future. Go ahead and write how you want to take the grandkids camping although your firstborn has yet to come. Set a goal to pay off your parents' mortgage in spite of your bank account being in the three-digit category, *including* the zeros after the decimal point. Having these types of goals alongside your purpose is another way to remind you how important it is to not only excel in your purpose and potential, but to appreciate it with the ones around you.

Influential

The most important thing to realize is that you must position yourself within your purpose and use it to influence our society in a positive way.

If you have not figured it out yet, I am not that big on finances because monetary value can always be met if you focus on being a person of influence. If you can make enough noise in this world with your purpose, the money will come. Back to the Hierarchy of Needs, it is in the spiritual position that meets both the physiological and emotional needs as well. Although your influential goals could have a number on them, the most important thing to realize is that you must position yourself within your purpose and use it to influence our society in a positive way.

There was an interview on Tyler Perry that I saw not too long ago and the conversation on his wealth-building success came up. The man stated that money was never the goal. All he wanted to do was make plays that people could relate to so they know that they are not alone. Here is a man who was at one point homeless, keeping his purpose in mind at all times and his influential goals a part of it. It was in that mindset that the finances came rolling in and he went from having nothing to owning a multi-million dollar home in Atlanta, among other things.

Your influential goals should always be about others and not about you. The goal is to better people through your purpose, not let your purpose be an asset to your bank account. The bank account will come if you focus on the latter.

Experimental

Trying out new things and placing yourself in environments that you are not accustomed to will help you put things in a different perspective.

Experimental goals are the goals that are outside the box. These goals are based on pure curiosity and designed to create new ideas by being in a different universe. Not too long ago I took a trip to Alaska with my singing group and experienced the wonders of nature. Born and raised in a city that put the New York City skyline in my backyard made me more accustomed to concrete and rats than trees and bugs. What I got out of being in Alaska was more than I could have ever found at home because it was a whole new world. From zip lining to hiking, my eyes were opened to something that I would have never come across if I just lived life as usual. It was in that process that I really learned how much I appreciated writing and there are fragments of this book that date back to my time in the wild.

Trying out new things and placing yourself in environments that you are not accustomed to will help you put things in a different perspective. As long as you continually have your purpose in mind, new ideas will come rushing simply because you are no longer in your usual habitat.

Goals all come back to your purpose in life. It is in these goals that you can have a baseline for the person that you want to be when you are sitting at your own garden party decades down the road.

It is time to see how far we can go by understanding our potential within our purpose and setting the first bar we must climb over.

Key Points

- The issue is not the number of talents you have to implement your purpose, it is the effort you put into those talents that is most important.
- Goals are dreams with a measurement and a deadline.
- The concept that knowledge is power is very true as long as the knowledge sinks in and is put into action.
- The reason family is a part of our *what* is because many of us will forget to enjoy the people we love the most if we do not include them in our goals.
- It is important to not only excel in your purpose and potential, but to appreciate it with the ones around you.
- The most important thing to realize is that you must position yourself within your purpose and use it to influence our society in a positive way.

Digging Deeper

Fill in the blanks of the equation for your purpose statement is:

I, _____, will represent [insert values _____] by [lost discovery _____], [open discovery _____], and [expertise discovery _____].

Giving 100 percent effort to accomplishing your tasks is what renders the most **of you** as well as the most **for you**. Look at the goal setting categories and fill in the key statements from each one. Then list your personal goals under each one.

Educational: *The education you desire should _____ the track you are _____ on so it can match the track your _____ is on.*

Family: *The reason family is a part of our what is because many of us will forget to enjoy the people we love the most if we do not include them in our goals. It is important to not only excel in your purpose and potential, but to appreciate it with the ones around you.*

Influential: *You must position yourself within your purpose and use it to _____ our society in a _____ way. The goal is to _____ people through your _____, _____ let your purpose just be an asset to your _____ _____.*

Experimental: *Trying out new things and placing yourself in environments that you are not accustomed to will help you puts things in a _____ _____.*

It is time to see how far we can go by understanding our potential within our purpose and setting the first bar we must climb over. Are you ready?

Chapter 7

Doubt

*D*oing Everything to Exceed your Potential *is the idea that the pinnacle of your existence relies on you raising the bar and reaching new levels as often as you possibly can. In order to achieve this goal you must realize that your strength is inside of you. In other words, you need to tap into your potential.

Potential

Potential *is a funky word that gets thrown around a lot in our world, leading to very similar, but also very different interpretations.* **Our definition is** *someone or something that has the capability of exceeding what would naturally and/or stereotypically be anticipated. Let's take it a little further.*

Capacity *is in terms of space or room to fill. The reason this specific word is used as part of the definition of potential is due to its connotations. "Room to fill" implies that the area is already there and all that we must do as individuals is stuff it with the information we acquire from life. This is fitting to our idea that all of our answers are within us due to the Higher Power that coincides in us all. All that we must do is continuously* **dig deep** *within ourselves to discover how close in relation we are to this world we live in.*

***Exceed** is to go beyond limitations and overcoming them. We all are capable of more than we imagine, but we tend to limit ourselves with our doubts and excuses. Although the limitations are more of a mirage, they seem real to us because we tell ourselves they are. Stinkin' thinkin', remember? We must overcome those limitations. The following chapters will discuss how to not only overcome current limitations, but the ones that will be in the future as well.*

The words **naturally** and **stereotypically** correspond to the nature versus nurture battle crusade. There are certain boundaries that we believe are there simply because they have not happened yet so if it comes to pass, it is something extraordinary. Let's take running the forty-yard dash as an example of a **natural boundary**. If someone ran the forty-yard dash tomorrow with a time of 4.0 seconds, the world would be in shock and awe because it has never happened. (The fastest time recorded time is 4.12 seconds.) In nature, that seems like an impossible feat due to the physical stress that such speed would put on the human body. The laws of physics negate its possibility so it is naturally "impossible."

On the other hand, **stereotypical** disbelief would be similar to Senator Barack Obama's election to presidency. Although it is technically not impossible in nature for an African-American male to become President, the probability of such a feat was high because up until that point only white males had been elected as Presidents. We will face one or both of these combatants and will have to defeat them as we move to achieve our full potential.

Anticipation is a word that is vital when referencing potential because that is what makes it so exhilarating. It is not the surprise that makes potential great. It is anticipating and hoping for the surprise that transforms everything. It is similar to the difference between a soap opera and a scary movie. When watching a soap opera, we go along without a drastic shift in the plot that draws us into an almost complacent loop. Our lack of expectancy is what puts us in a more vulnerable position to be surprised by the change in scenario and then we say, "I did not expect that." However, we all think we "know" what is going to happen in a scary movie, so we sit on the edge of our seats and prepare ourselves for someone to jump out of the shadows. Then when they come up out of the floor we say, "I expected something, but I was not expecting *that!*" Progress within our purpose by reaching our potential may be expected, but when we take it to a different place than most contemplate, we are in the world of anticipation.

So the definition of potential, when we *really* break it down, is someone or something that has the space or capacity within to go beyond the limitations of what has yet been done with the hope of a prize that surpasses what was anticipated. Our potential then is directly related to how far we can go with our purpose in life.

But Jesus looked at them and said to them, "With men this is impossible, but with God all things are possible. (Matthew 19:26)

In Pursuit of Happiness

One of the reasons so many of us are not satisfied with our lives is because we are not living up to our full potential. The United States Declaration of Independence states that we have the right to life, liberty, and the *pursuit* of happiness. Isn't it peculiar that happiness is the only thing on that list that involves a call to action? Life and liberty are our inalienable rights that we have due to our existence, but happiness is something that we must make for ourselves both mentally and physically. It is acquired by our efforts to move towards our calling. Happiness is found when life revolves around the success of our purpose. We do so by constantly seeking to exceed our potential.

We all go through four phases in our pursuit of happiness and seeking to exceed our potential.

- Doubt
- Excuses
- Engagement
- Performance

Whether we are deciding on a place to eat or starting our own company, we all have a conversation with the voice(s) in our head to decide if, and/or when we will take action. We first question the thought that comes to mind. The lack of confidence we have in ourselves, along with the lack of faith from others tells us that we cannot choose. **Doubt** says it is a "stupid idea" or it "can never happen." We go from saying we cannot choose to saying we cannot *do* because we doubt our ability to achieve our purpose. Our inability to establish a balance between priority and comfort directs us to make **excuses** to explain our inactivity. Both the doubt and excuse phases are defeated by digging deep into the purpose of our purpose using the material we have established as important in the previous chapters. Our "whys" push us towards mental success to break through the threshold taking us from inactivity to activity. Crossing that threshold takes us from mental to physical, making dreams turn into goals and putting our plans to action.

Both the doubt and excuse phases are defeated by digging deep into the purpose of our purpose using the material we have established as important in the previous chapter.

As soon as we reach **engagement**, we must make our way through the arc of influence and dig even deeper into who we are inside. We go from barely surviving and hanging on by a thread in our purpose, to a person of significance via our **performance** at the highest level. How do we get to where we perform at the highest level? We do so by exceeding our potential. **Doubts** and **Excuses** live within our mental behavior and actions with **Engagement** and **Performance** exists in our physical behavior. It is in our habits that we create success as we move through each phase and go from being inactive to proactive.

Inactive to Proactive

This is a process that we excel in by proactively grounding ourselves and digging deeper and deeper into our purpose by looking for the smallest gem(s) possible to reach another place in our potential. In doing so, the world *reactively* places the success and wealth we all desire in every aspect of our lives. By consciously making the effort to change our mental behavior, we can create the habits necessary to build the character required to sustain the accolades given in response. Once we succeed in shifting our mental behavior, we engage in our purpose to launch the shift in our physical behavior. Choosing between the things we want now and the things we want most in life is a muscle that gets stronger by going for the most, regularly.

Behavior does not change overnight. It will be painful at first to wake up earlier and work harder, but our bodies crave whatever we put in them. We are either taught or we teach ourselves what we desire and crave. It is something we feed into our behavior by consistently acting on the desired change which leads to the formation of new mental and physical habits.

What a paradox it would be to find someone that became an alcoholic just by osmosis. One becomes an alcoholic by first seeing themselves capable of drinking (mentally) and then (physically) acting on their mental behavior. After continuously having their mental thoughts become physical actions, their body *then* attaches itself to the substance. We first become slaves mentally with our thoughts, then physically with our actions, *then* physiologically with the headaches and detoxing.

As a man thinks in his heart so he is. (Proverbs 23:7 NKJV)

The same applies with purpose and having the desire to exceed and reach toward attaining our potential. We must first sacrifice our mental behavior and shift our thought process so our actions, whether in reaction or not, make our physical behavior dependent on our purpose. Then we can finally reach our goal where our physical bodies cannot help but apply our purpose in life. Our bodies naturally inhale knowledge and positive habits to rejuvenate the cells that help us dig deep so it can exhale the work done within our purpose subconsciously. We pro-act and our body then re-acts in that manner. This is how we shift from our purpose being what we do to who we are. So are you ready for the detox? It's not going to be pretty.

Doubt is the one thing that has killed more purposes, dreams, and goals than anything else on the planet.

DOUBT
*"Whether you think you can,
or you think you can't–you're right."*
(Henry Ford)

Doubt is the one thing that has killed more purposes, dreams, and goals than anything else on the planet. The casualties are exponential and its sole desire is to prevent you from acting on anything that you can imagine. Almost anything that you can think of doing is almost always shot down first by doubt. By definition, doubt is to be uncertain, lack belief or faith. It comes from fearing the unknown and focusing more on what has been as oppose to what could be. Basically, you do not believe in it because there is no physical evidence to make you believe.

One of the first things that a person says when they confront something that they hesitate to believe is "prove it to me." They want some form of representation that they can comprehend in order to agree that what is being presented is real. In science, you do so by testing the subject over and over again. In job hunting, you have an elaborate resume and the proper responses during the interview. As a student you make it happen with better grades and attitude. As a husband it is paying more attention and showing that you care by spending quality time with your wife. All in all, you clear doubt with results. Easier said than done though, right?

The process of creating is the most difficult thing we can do as human beings, but it is imperative for growth and to make purpose a reality.

There are three types of doubt that all of us must overcome in order to take the next step in digging deep. Each of us must overcome the doubt from our superiors, from society, and from ourselves in order to get to the next step—in order to even make the next step.

As I write this book, I am constantly hearing the whispers of unforeseen beings that want to do anything but let me achieve my goals. They squawk and cackle questions that the Devil (pitchfork and all) manufactures in the depths of Hell. They are designed to rise above the smog of his lair to pollute the world by destroying any possible force of positivity as he attempts to stop the train from ever leaving the station. Is it any wonder we fight within ourselves so intensely when dealing with a purposeful decision that can make the world a better place and make ourselves better people? Not doing anything is just as much a victory for the evil in this world as being a part of the evil.

Doubting is somewhat inevitable and everyone goes through a phase of doubt whenever they are making a decision. Some of us doubt even after the decision is made, all because of the voices in our heads. Every "can't" and "I don't think so" that arrives is designed to protect us, but when it comes to purpose, doubt from within is designed to prevent us. The difference between this doubt and the others that we will speak about is how impossible it is to avoid. No matter what we do, the only way to overcome self-doubt is by confronting it head-to-head, and dealing with its desire to keep us in the same place and living life as usual. Our greatest enemy always has and always will be the person we see in the mirror.

When our adversary comes at us with doubt, it comes in these ways:

- Uncertainty
- Unfamiliarity
- Looking Too Far (Ahead OR Behind)
- Plausibility

One of these four reasons will always come up when doubt is involved. The logic behind each of them is valid when we focus on the things we can currently see, but do not even scratch the surface on what we foresee. Society, superiors, and ourselves may administer one of the four agents of doubt, but it is up to us to overlook and overcome them by faith. Faith positions itself to give us the power to act.

> *Let perseverance finish its work so that you may be mature and complete, not lacking anything. If any of you lacks wisdom, you should ask God, who gives generously to all without finding fault, and it will be given to you. But when you ask, you must believe and not doubt, because the one who doubts is like a wave of the sea, blown and tossed by the wind. That person should not expect to receive anything from the Lord. Such a person is double-minded and unstable in all they do.* (James 1:4-8 NIV)

Key Points

- The definition of potential is someone or something that has the space within to go beyond the limitations of what has yet been done with the hope of a prize that surpasses what was anticipated.

- Our potential is directly related to how far we can go with our purpose in life.
- Both the doubt and excuse phases are defeated by digging deep into the purpose of our purpose using the material we have established as important in the previous chapter.
- Doubt is the one thing that has killed more purposes, dreams, and goals than anything else on the planet.
- The process of creating is the most difficult thing we can do as human beings, but it is imperative for growth and to make purpose a reality.
- Our greatest enemy always has and always will be the person we look at in the mirror.

Digging Deeper

When our adversary comes at us with doubt, it comes in these ways. Look these over, write out a definition of each one, and see which ones your adversary has been using against you causing you to doubt:

- Uncertainty
- Unfamiliarity
- Looking Too Far (Ahead OR Behind)
- Plausibility

How important is it that you overcome doubt? (Read James 1:4-8.)

Chapter 8

Self-Doubt

Next to "trust falls," one of my least favorite games for team building is when they blindfold you and have a partner guide you somewhere "safely." The idea of entrusting my life to another individual is just one of the craziest things...ever. We have all been there. You put your hands out in front of you as you shuffle your feet like the walking dead, hoping that stairs and low ceilings are *not* a part of the equation. What is definitely a part of the equation is uncertainty because you are walking blind. More people would choose to be deaf than to go blind because everything is unknown when you no longer have sight.

Self-doubt puts an emphasis on uncertainty because you cannot see what the future holds. Due to the fact that you are walking into unchartered territory within your purpose, you do not get to see what tomorrow holds. There is no security in past experiences. There is no recollection of what has happened before. Each step taken is based on hope and faith. The reason you can trust your purpose and continue to walk the path is due to your insight. You may not have sight, but you do have vision. To depict yourself as the person you are striving to be is half the battle. Seeing the result(s) you want to have in your mind's eye once all is final is how you can ignore the fact that your literal eyes have no viewing of what is to come. That is why it is so important to work *from the end* and not *to the end*. Setting your goals ahead of you gives you a point of focus to clearly visualize your future.

Where there is no vision, the people perish. (Proverbs 29:18 KJV)

One of the best things I have ever read came from an article about Walt Disney. As the story goes, Walt never actually "saw" Disney World. His passing came before its debut, leading many people to ask what he would have said during its release. This led to one of his partners stating, *"WALT DID SEE IT!"* From the park to the plethora of new content thereafter, there were many things that Walt Disney never had the chance to see with his eyes, but he had seen them in his mind and believed in his heart that they will come to exist. The idea is very similar to a puzzle. When you have the hundreds of pieces all over the place *without* that box with a picture of what should be the end result, it sets you up for failure right from the start. You probably will not even make the attempt because there is nothing to move toward. That is why the big picture is so invaluable. It gives you vision and shifts uncertainty to probability.

Setting your goals ahead of you gives you a point of focus to clearly visualize your future.

Cristofo Colombo
In fourteen hundred ninety-two
Columbus sailed the ocean blue.

The definition of unfamiliarity is Christopher Columbus. Up to this point, people still believed the Earth was flat. If you went beyond the horizon, your life would have seen its last horizon, but this man had *insight*. Although he was unfamiliar with what lay ahead in his journey, he was familiar with the one thing that is vital in purpose and that was *himself*. He knew what he believed and decided to go after it when the opportunity presented itself. He entrusted the time and energy he had to study and plan to exceed his potential in understanding geography and how the world was designed to take on the purpose he had envisioned.

When my group auditioned for NBC's *The Sing Off*, we were definitely unfamiliar with the situation. The Voices of Lee is an acapella group from a Christian university smaller than a lot of public high schools, and yet we were auditioning to be on national television. The way we fought the unfamiliar ground was with preparation. Every day for the fifteen years prior, the Voices of Lee would practice two hours *every single day* and perform almost every weekend. (And believe me when I say that our rehearsals were not for the faint of heart.) From the courthouse to the church house, VOL would go wherever they would be received and rendered their best when doing so. Every single day we were together singing, in and outside of the practice room. A few of the members actually lived with me in my home in Tennessee for years, making the word family more fitting for us because we were always together.

Now we do not know how, when, nor why the wonderful folk of NBC got word of us, but they did and we were ready. All of that work up until that point might have seemed pointless, but the day finally came when the point of it all became clear that day in the audition room in front of those producers.

"Luck is when preparation and opportunity crosses paths" is what our director told us, and we definitely had one half of that equation ready.

We did exceptionally well during the audition giving us the opportunity to be on the inaugural season of The Sing Off, but our victory lap started when we sang our very first note back in 1994. It is inevitable to hit unfamiliar waters like Christopher Columbus when you are going after your dreams. When you work your tail off up to that moment where your preparation intersects opportunity, you look at what is unfamiliar as the only thing that separates you from greatness. If you know that greatness is just on the other side, it does not matter what tries to come in between.

The Big Picture

It is a marathon, not a sprint.

When I was twelve years old, I was about 5'7" and weighed about 260 pounds. Needless to say, I wanted to play football when I started high school. When I got to pre-season though, I wanted to do everything but. The first few days all we did was use the word, run—run plays, run drills, run and then run. Doing this three times a day in the heat of August did not make this scene any more bearable. Before the first week was out I was worn down and preparing to give it up. I did not think I would make it to the end of the day, let alone to the actual season that would include daily practices *and* school.

Luckily, one of my coaches saw how I was inching closer to defeat and throwing in the towel so he pulled me to the side. He told me how looking at the big picture can sometimes bring us more harm than good because it is so big. It makes the goals impossible and the dream implausible.

"You have got to take it day by day, practice by practice, snap by snap" he told me. "That is the only way to beat something that you have never seen before."

That one conversation changed my life forever. I did survive pre-season and played football all throughout my high school career, but there is more to this story than football. One of the reasons we doubt ourselves is because we look too far into the distance. For me, it was looking too far ahead as I was freaking about homework and morning workouts before we even had a practice with full pads.

After setting the big picture before you, it can be dangerous to keep that as the focus day in and out. Its enormity brings in more fear and doubt than you might have had before. This is because you are looking at your purpose when you have yet to reach your first position. Your long-term goals will not seem tangible to your current position. Even if the goal is weeks out, the person you will grow to be in those weeks will be a much bigger and better person than the one you are at the present time. In all actuality, if you want more, you have to be more. There are moments in your journey that require you to look down at your feet as you take each step as opposed to focusing on the prize that is far off in the distance. Remember that your potential and your purpose are *yours* for a reason. It is there for you to excel in. As the old proverb goes, it is a marathon, not a race. Pace yourself and take it day by day, practice by practice, snap by snap.

Science Fact vs. Science Fiction

As a kid (and embarrassingly still as an "adult") I read comics and sci-fi books. I love how people portray the future and all of the cool technology they dream up. I love it all the more now within the last millennia as they have taken such great writing and made them into movies. One of them that I like to watch is *Thor*. In the movie, there is a debate between two scientists about who this guy, Thor, is because up to this point, they just know him as a man that they hit with their car as oppose to a demigod. The argument goes as follows:

Erik Selvig: "I just wanted to show you how silly his story was."

Jane Foster: "But you're the one who's always pushing me to chase down every possibility, every alternative."

Erik Selvig: "I'm talking about science, not magic."

Jane Foster: "Well, 'magic's just science we don't understand yet.' Arthur C. Clarke."

Self-Doubt

<u>Erik Selvig</u>: "Who wrote science-fiction."

<u>Jane Foster</u>: "A precursor to science fact!"

Science-fiction is a precursor to science fact? All of us who love science-fiction and superheroes know just about every bit of technology we have today was written about decades ago in novels and stories. From laser guns to cell phones, they have been thought of and depicted as either magic or science fiction. Although some doubted their possibilities as reality, others decided to take the chance and see if these ideas could literally jump off the pages.

Plausibility is based on perception. If you believe in your heart that it will be then it will. The only thing that is preventing it from it being science fact is time and effort.

In knowing this, it can be said that the only difference between science fact and science fiction is time. Time has and always will be the *only thing* that separates the impossible from the possible.

- Do not doubt yourself or your dreams simply because they have not happened yet.
- Do not be uncertain of your potential because they are only words for the time being.
- Do not hesitate just because no one has done it before.

The reason no one else has done it before may be because *you* are supposed to be the first person to do it. Plausibility is based on perception. If you believe in your heart that it will be then it will. The only thing that is preventing it from it being science fact is time and *your* effort.

Be a Race Horse

In essence, self-doubt comes when you look around you as oppose to within you.

As stated earlier, you have all the tools within you to achieve anything you set your mind to. Your purpose has been designated for you and you alone, making your potential within it not only a possibility, but a duty. Everything has been laid out before you to better both your life and our society. Whether you like it or not, you were born for this and the only way to have faith within yourself is to have some animal instincts similar to a thorough bred race horse.

1. *Born for Greatness*: A race horse is not just any old pony that comes from the barn. No, these bad boys are bred. They come from this type of horse and that type of horse to become the great creatures that they are, and you were created the same way. Who you are, where you come from, and what you have been through have a part in your purpose. The greatness that is discovered within yourself by exceeding your potential came into existence the same time you hopped out the womb, if not sooner. A race horse knows only to be what it is—a race horse. Whatever your purpose is, that is what defines you and that is the only thing that needs to matter in terms of your identity. So strap in and discover the greatness inside.
2. *Work at it Every Day*: A race horse does one thing every single day and that is train to be a race horse. When you work on your purpose daily, you begin to build the faith needed to move the mountains ahead. You expect to fear the unknown and the only way to change the scenario is by changing your relationship with the unknown. Get acclimated to it by looking into it each day and see how doubt begins to pass away as well.

Self-Doubt

3. *You Are Who You Say You Are:* Even before their first race, a race horse is considered a race horse. Due to the fact that they are bred, the decades that have been put into these creatures before they are even born tells you that they are going to be a race horse. We often are doubtful because we try to replace our identity and purpose with that of someone else's. A race horse cannot be a show horse or a horse that takes you around Times Square. If the horse is incapable of racing, they get shot and thrown in a ditch somewhere.

   Now we may not literally do that to you, but it happens spiritually. There is no coincidence that zombie movies are so popular. When we work a job or have a major in school that was not designed for our purpose and is counterproductive to our potential, we feel dead inside as we live our "miserable lives". We each are created to be something very specific for our world and it is only in going after that purpose that we can truly live. Mind you, the person you are supposed to be is within you, so you are technically that individual. There may be a lot more to learn and much more ground to cover to reach that moment in your potential, but that person in inside of you. The world may not know it yet, but time will tell them otherwise.

4. *Put in Your Mouthpiece*: It amazes me how you can control such a big thing like a horse just by putting in a mouthpiece and reigns. What you say to and about yourself will make or break your future. Be positive and put in your mouthpiece to avoid anything less.

5. *Throw on Blinders*: Blinders for a horse does not actually "blind" them, but it closes in their sight to keep them focused on what is ahead. Sometimes you have to duck your head down and just focus on putting in the work. Do not look to the left or the right, do not pass go and do not collect $200. Tunnel vision is in this case a positive.

6. *Do Not Forget Your Horseshoes*: The reason race horses have horseshoes is because they are not meant to be moving that fast for such an extended period of time, nor on the terrain that they travel on. You have to acknowledge the unchartered territory you are about to walk in and know that you will be walking in it for a long time. This means that you must prepare yourself for what you are hoping to come. Luck is when preparation meets opportunity. Character is what sustains success. Put on the proper footwear that will help you endure and excel the journey laid out before you.

Prepare yourself for the opportunity by growing and honing in on your strengths consistently and soon you will see that your efforts will not be in vain.

> *By failing to prepare,*
> *you are preparing to fail.*
> -Benjamin Franklin

Key Points

- Setting your goals ahead of you gives you a point of focus to clearly visualize your future.
- Luck is when preparation and opportunity crosses paths.
- Plausibility is based on perception. If you believe in your heart that it will be then it will. The only thing that is preventing it from it being science fact is time and effort.
- In essence, self-doubt comes when you look around you as oppose to *within* you.
- Prepare yourself for the opportunity by growing and honing in on your strengths consistently and soon you will see that your efforts will not be in vain.

Digging Deeper

Time has and always will be the *only thing* that separates the impossible from the possible. Look at this do not list and make sure you understand what it is telling you about your own personal journey.

- Do not doubt yourself or your dreams simply because they have not happened yet.
- Do not be uncertain of your potential because they are only words for the time being.
- Do not hesitate just because no one has done it before.

Here is your Be Like a Race Horse Check-off List. Check them off if you have dealt with that step. Then go back and work on the ones you have not checked off.

p *Born for Greatness*: Who you are, where you come from, and what you have been through have a part in your purpose. Whatever your purpose is that is what defines you and that is the only thing that needs to matter in terms of your identity so strap in and discover the greatness inside. Now declare and believe you are born for greatness!

p *Work at it Every Day*: When you work on your purpose daily, you begin to build the faith needed to move the mountains ahead. You expect to fear the unknown and the only way to change the scenario is by changing your relationship with the unknown. Are you working on it daily?

p *You Are Who You Say You Are:* We often are doubtful because we try to replace our identity and purpose with that of someone else's. Who are you?

p *Put in Your Mouthpiece*: What you say to and about yourself will make or break your future. Be positive and put in your mouthpiece to avoid anything less. Track your self-talk for one day and see where you need to adjust how you talk to yourself.

p *Throw on Blinders*: Sometimes you have to duck your head down and just put in the work. Do not look to the left or the right, do not pass go and do not collect $200. Tunnel vision is in this case a positive. Track how you used your energy today. What was your primary focus?

p *Do Not Forget Your Horseshoes*: You have to acknowledge the unchartered territory you are about to walk in and know that you will be walking in it for a long time. What does the terrain look like where you are going on your journey?

p Prepare yourself for the opportunity by growing and honing in on your strengths consistently and soon you will see that your efforts will not be in vain.

Chapter 9

Societal Doubt

The next form of doubt is societal. Now this form of doubt technically involves *everyone*. Society, simply defined, is a group of people living together as a community. This community can be as small as your immediate family or as big as the Earth itself. Each size is a part of a world that you live in, and by default you have to be a part of it.

Influential Circles of Society

For our purposes, there are four circles of society that we will be speaking about.

- Family
- Friends
- Familiars
- Folks

Each one has their reasons for doubting you when you start this journey and some of these doubts are valid. It is your job to figure out where these doubts are coming from, understand the doubter's perspective, process it, and then let it go. The only way you change the mind of others is when you do what you are called to do and fulfill your purpose. With that in mind, here are some analogies that will help you determine the perspective of your doubter.

1. ***Mother Hen*** – The outspoken, overprotective, worrier caregiver.

This person in your family does not mean any harm when you introduce them to your dreams. On the contrary, they want to protect you from them and that is why they doubt. Now, just to clarify, mother hen *can be* male or female, but I will use *she* throughout this explanation simply because a mother and a hen are both female (and I may be biased as a male).

A mother hen does not want you to be heartbroken or defeated, so they want you to take the safe route for everything. Knowing the scale of your purpose (which should and always be gargantuan), she knows that you must give it all you got, but also knows she cannot come to your aide in any way, shape or form because this is your fight to win. What we must understand is that mother hen only wants the best and will do all she can for that to happen. When facing this kind of future, she knows her hands are tied which leads her to doubt.

2. ***Going Down Memory Lane*** – The hysterically historical with the memory of an elephant

There is *always* someone in your life that wants to bring up *every single negative* thing that has happened to you in the past to persuade you to change your mind. This person is sometimes doing this for your good and other times they are not. No matter their reasoning, *you* must plant your feet in the present and keep your eyes on the future. Remember that your past does not define you. Just remind yourself how you closed that previous chapter in your life, and be ready to start the next one.

3. ***Marcia, Marcia, Marcia!*** - The jealous insecure one

Back in the '70s, there was a show called *The Brady Bunch*. This family sitcom was a story about a lovely lady and a man named

Societal Doubt

Brady with their six kids, nanny, and dog. In the show, the middle daughter, Jan, would always complain that her oldest sister, Marcia, got all the attention. In essence, she was jealous. There are going to be *plenty* of people (both in and outside of your family) that will be jealous of you when you are heading towards your potential. It is important that you just keep on keeping on with what you are doing and ignore them because time and energy spent on trying to counteract their jealousy is pointless.

4. ***This is the Diary of...*** - They *think* they know everything about you

"You think you know, but you have *no idea.*" This phrase comes from the MTV show *Diary*. The show goes "inside lives" of well-known celebrities to show you who they are as people, not just performers. There will be *a lot* of people that think they know you better than you know yourself. Some of these people you may have known your entire life, but that does not change the fact that where you are today is not where you were yesterday. So even if they do "know you" today, they do not know "the you" of tomorrow. They have not seen who you will become...but you have. You know that person at the garden party and you know what must be done to achieve your purpose and exceed your potential. It is now time to act on it.

5. ***Here Comes a New Challenger*** - Player 2 just hit the START button

The best form of doubt out of all of these (if there is one) is the doubt that challenges you. Just like any of those old arcade fighting games, this person doubts you because they want to see what you got. It is good old fashioned competition that is there to make you stronger, even if the other party does not know it. One thing I *loathe* is when my friends come at me with the phrase "bet you won't." The *only* reason they put those words together and in that order is so I will do whatever it is they say I "can't" do because they know that I am (extremely) competitive. Something in me just wants to prove them wrong and show them that I can. It frustrates me because they know I can, but they want me to *show them*. Given the circumstances of changing your life, go ahead and prove to them that not only *can* you do it, but you already *are* doing it by taking steps with this book.

Outside Looking In

Overall, the big thing about societal doubt is that most of it comes from people looking from the outside in. They do not really know what you are capable of and do not know what you are willing to do. A lot of them do not even understand what it means to not only reach your potential, but to exceed your potential as you make your purpose in life become your life. They have not had the courage to do it themselves. We can only perceive things through the lens in which we can perceive ourselves. It is your job to open their eyes to hope and prosperity by doing it *within yourself* first as you bring it closer to their reality.

> *"Work until your superiors are looking at you dead in the eyes."*
> - Philip Bonaparte

There will *always* be someone above you that doubts you. For our purposes, the word *superior* can be defined as someone who has authority over you. This can range from a professor you are wanting the superior grade from, to the bank you are trying to get a loan with. These people have the capability of being the blockades between you and where you want to be. The most important thing to recognize with the doubts of superiors is the validity of their doubt. Unlike the doubt from within or the doubt from society, these people will *always* have a legitimate reason for doubting you (or so they say). Superior doubt will always be based off of them doing their job. We all have watched a movie where a character will say, "I was just doing my job." This is just another way of saying that what they have done is not personal and they are just following protocol. Now do not get me wrong, there are definitely a few individuals that use their authority for personal reasons, but that is beside the point. Their personal vendetta with you is something that you may never be capable of fixing, but you *can fix* any doubt that is based from their status in relation to you through experience, protection, and counsel.

Educated Guess

My father has been a medical doctor for over twenty years now and is a man of wonders. The day I can shine his shoes will be the moment success could be in the same sentence as my name. He is one of the most intelligent people I know and has a heart only second to my mother. As a doctor, he has had to diagnose multiple patients and figured out their problem at a moment's notice. If he does not then someone's life is *literally* on the line.

Throughout my life I have heard him talk about the countless doctors misdiagnosing people and almost killing them. After hearing this time and time again, I asked myself the million-dollar question, *why*? What I have discovered has not only helped me when facing the doubt of someone above me, but has also helped me with my own personal doubt because it makes that much sense. So this is a two-for-one.

Physicians are considered to be world-class in the field of medicine. Just like any other world-class individual, there is something that separates them from others. What is the difference? Is it education? Experience? Student loan debt? Here's the "Bottom Line:" *what separates people from being world-class is time.* Their time in that specific field is the only thing that makes your answer look foolish and theirs look God-sent. Actually, that is the *only* difference between you and anybody that is considered a "professional" or an "expert." It goes back to the adage that it takes at least 10,000 hours for anyone to be an expert at anything. Having the title of expert does not mean that that person is always right, although it is often implied.

Just because you walk into their stale smelling office of out-of-date magazines, patiently wait to explain your symptoms in much detail to the physician *after* patiently waiting again in the actual examining room of bright white lights and awkwardly thin paper that you must sit on with as much comfort as grandmother's couch that still has the plastic over it, does not mean that what they tell you is *right*. What they tell you in the end, when you boil it down, is an *educated guess*. They will not be sure until you go and take the less than tasteful medication they give you, take more tests, have a follow-up evaluation, and possibly another *educated guess* until there is a match between you, your symptoms, and their answer. It is basically a glorified version of trying to find out which answer is right in the multiple choice section of your math test by process of elimination.

Now, do not get me wrong, they definitely have a lot more background with the situation and have a better probability of being correct, but it is still a probability.

Malcolm Gladwell wrote a book about this called *Blink*. The book took a look into first impressions and initial responses as the question "how did you know" continuously resonates. It is an understanding that you cannot understand how or why you respond to something when you are at an expert level in the blink of an eye. The beauty of that is what cannot be computed also cannot be set in stone *until* it is proven.

So what does that have to do with you? If you are going to the bank for a loan on that new building you need for your company or you are not given that internship opportunity, their doubt in you does not have to be the doubt *for* you. They are simply taking an educated guess on who you are based on their past experiences with someone similar. It is a simple way to remove the factor of individuality out of every scenario. It is your job to force that individuality on them because your uniqueness is the very reason they *should* believe in you. All in all, just prove them wrong.

You must also go ahead and seek the help and advice from others, though. Going back to doctors, you are supposed to get the opinions of two to three doctors whenever you are in need of a diagnosis. There is nothing more important than your dream becoming a reality so you must do whatever you have to do for that to be true. Your belief in your success is just as valid as their belief in your failure because the only difference is their educated guess is in relation to their experience while your belief is in the education you know *within* yourself.

Close The Gates!

Another reason why your superiors may doubt you is for protection purposes. This protection is a little different from Mother Hen's. This protection is not *for* you, but *from* you. Now there are two reasons for this. They do not believe you can achieve your purpose or they are afraid that you *will* achieve, making you their competition. Back in the day when cities and towns were hedged by stones reaching for the skies, there would be a very big gate in front of the city. This gate would be used to protect the city and its citizens from anything that posed a threat to the community. The king of the land would simply have guards stationed there to stop the "small" threats from doing anything. If anyone out of town wanted to get into the city, they would have to explain why they wanted to be there and why they should be let in. Along with the soldiers, some gates would have carvings and insignias on their towering walls to scare off people that could be a threat.

Standing in front of the gates that could possibly help you with your objectives can definitely be intimidating. Walking through them and explaining why your superiors should put their trust in you is even more frightening. You must remember that your fear at that moment is only a small relapse in the self-doubt category, so remind yourself *why* you are there and look within, not without.

Although they are there to scare you off, you cannot let their agenda be yours. These people are "just doing their job" and are there to protect themselves and their organization.

Now on the other hand, they could also be there because you pose an *actual* threat to them. They are not trying to scare you, but are trying to take you out because they think you are not "as strong" as they are yet. Just like doubt from society, you have to remember that their reality is not yours. You are as strong as them and they should be afraid. So, if they want to close the gates on you then you have to get your battering ram and knock that bad boy down! If a door can close then it can also open, and that could happen from either side.

Either way, to prove yourself you must not only meet their expectations or beliefs in you, but *surpass* them. The way you do that will be discussed later on in the book and you will be prepared to do so. Until then, just remember that if someone can close the gates then you can also open them when you have the right amount of effort.

Yet Another Challenger

I am convinced that my mentor Danny Murray *loved* to use his superiority to challenge people. He had a knack for finding a sore spot and digging into it until you took action. His doubt in you was more like hope in disguise, but you definitely felt as if you did not have a chance. This form of doubt is in the category of *character building*. The only reason a superior would put you through this gauntlet is to build you up, as opposed to the typical belief that it puts you down. It is more of a realistic approach to growth because the real world does *not* withhold any blows.

One night when I was watching a documentary before a Floyd Mayweather fight, he was talking about his boxing coach, Floyd Mayweather, Sr. If any person closed their eyes and listened to these two have a conversation, you would think that they hated each other. Here you have an undefeated boxer, clearly one of the best, taking a verbal beat-down from his father. A beat-down that would make any man feel like a small, scrawny, school-boy that sat in the corner with the dunce-hat on their head. The doubt coming from Floyd Jr.'s superior was manufactured to make him a better fighter, although it could have made him feel like he was nothing.

The point of it all is to give a person an ultimatum. You either fold or you flourish. There will come a time when you have your back against the wall, feel helpless, and all your hope has been extracted from your being. As if all of this is not enough, there is a very dominant individual in front of you that is telling you that you will either live or die and that decision is made by you going through them. One of the reasons so many of us collapse under pressure is because we just are not used to being under it. This kind of pressure, although very real, is a part of your training that not only puts you at risk, but your superior as well.

They are rolling the dice right now with this challenge because it could be a giant leap forward. But that leap has a gap that could make you drop lower than you have ever been. What you must understand is that your superior is rolling the dice in *your favor*. They are putting all their chips in your corner and they want you to overcome the obstacle staring you in the eye. They want you to defeat it, not be defeated by it. So when your superior comes at you this way, you must ask yourself, *Am I going to fold or am I going to dig deep and flourish?*

Key Points

- Ñ Societal doubt comes from people looking from the outside in. They do not really know what you are capable of and do not know what you are willing to do.
- Ñ Actually, the *only* difference between you and anybody that is considered a "professional" or an "expert" is their experience. It takes at least 10,000 hours for anyone to be an expert at anything.

- Your belief in your success is just as valid as their belief in your failure because the only difference is their educated guess is based on their experience while your belief is in the education you know is *within* yourself.

Digging Deeper

Time to do some more self-evaluation.

- Do not worry about mother hen's fears because they are not relevant to you.
- Remember that your past does not define you.
- Just keep on keeping on with what you are doing and ignore those who are jealous because time and energy spent on trying to counteract their jealousy is pointless.
- Remind yourself *why* you are doing this as opposed to *who* you are doing this for.
- Go ahead and prove to them that not only *can* you do it, but you already *are* doing it!
- To prove yourself you must not only meet their expectations or beliefs in you, but *surpass* them.
- Ask yourself, *Am I going to fold or am I going to dig deep and flourish?*

Chapter 10

Facing & Confronting Doubts

Just remember that this is a fight that you can and must win.

Be a Boxer

There are a few components needed when facing the doubts of your superiors. These components are very similar to the needs of a world class boxer, so let's take a look at what they do to not only win a title, but keep one when in the ring.

1. *Offense* - There is no doubt (no pun intended) that you definitely need to know how to strike when you are dealing with the doubt of someone "superior" to you. Knowing how and when to attack is what makes boxing so difficult. So many people want to just run in there and start swinging, but that cannot happen. Most fighters understand that fatigue is what typically causes someone to lose. You must have a strategy, finesse and *patience* so you can charge at the opportune moment.
2. *Defense* - The blows will definitely be thrown back at you because no one wants to be a punching bag (not even a punching bag). If you are fast enough, dodging the swings is your best option because it not only clears you from

any damage, it makes your challenger more vulnerable. If you cannot dodge it, make sure to put your hands up and protect your purpose. But remember, it takes more energy to swing and miss than it is to make contact so do your best to have them do the latter. It not only weakens them physically, but it also hurts their morale mentally as they question their time spent preparing to defeat you.

3. *Endurance* - You do not know how tiring it is to be in a fight until you are actually in one. Throwing and taking blows is a workout and should not be taken lightly. What you must remember is that it is a war with many battles. They may win a few and that is okay. You have to be capable of just winning more. You cannot win more if you are not capable of making it through the entire bout. Stay strong and take your time.

4. *Counter* - When I play the game *Fight Night*, my *favorite* thing to do is counter. To counter someone (to me) is like walking up to them, looking them dead in their eyes, and smacking them in the face. You are basically saying, "I am going to hit you and there is nothing you can do about it." If you can make their doubts miss by not taking them to heart, all you have to do is come back and prove them wrong, which often leads to your victory and reveals their stupidity (for that moment at least).

5. *Finesse* - This one is probably *the most important* thing that any boxer could have. Finesse is control and wisdom with a bow on top. It is putting your strategy into action and *always* being on your agenda. It is knowing when you need to ram that gate with all you have got or when to regroup and come up with another plan. This is where fly like a butterfly and sting like a bee comes to play. You may have to change the plan sometimes, but never the goal.

6. *Faith* - One thing Muhammad Ali knew how to do was talk. This man wanted everyone to know that he was the best before he could prove it during the fight. It was a way

of making his superior, inferior. The reason why Ali had so much faith though is because he worked his butt off before every battle. If you believe in yourself as deep (and definitely as loud) as Muhammad Ali did for himself and put in the time and energy necessary to back it up, then you have won the match before you even take a step into the ring. If you can win the mental battle then the physical one will be a breeze.

Superior doubt is there to prove their authority over you. Their actions are a test of your character and an understanding of how important your purpose is. Just remember that this is a fight that you can and must win.

I hated every minute of training, but I said, 'Don't quit. Suffer now and live the rest of your life as a champion.' - Muhammad Ali

We Do Geometry

Before you try to skip this section because of the title, hear me out. I *know* many of us do not like math (and we will not be doing any of it so do not worry), but there are a lot of parallels between it and our lives. We all know that doubt comes from looking without as opposed to looking within. We all understand that it is something that takes courage to overcome because doubt is nothing more than a type of fear. Our fear comes from us looking at ourselves and thinking that none of it adds up. In all honesty, *it probably does not add up*. Instead of paying attention to that, you need to pay attention to this:

- Circle your purpose with prayers and hopes as you take it from 2-D to 3-D with high levels of performance.
- Do not be square in your thinking because imagination is the catalyst for innovation.

- Triangulate your goals because there will *always* be another way for you to reach them by changing the plan, *not* the goal.
- Dig deep into your purpose as you stay obtuse to let loose of your never ending potential (like pi because 3.14 is the *very* simplified version).
- Always look for parallels to make this life make sense.
- Graph out a plan, pin point your coordinates, and rise to the occasion as you run towards your goals because failing to prepare is how you prepare to fail.
- Know your angles and find ways for your goals to intersect with the goals of others because it is by giving that we receive.

A Mustard Seed

When a man wanted his son to be healed, he first confronted the disciples of Jesus Christ to do the miraculous. Their lack of faith lead to their failure and the need of Jesus to perform the miracle. When the disciples asked why they could not do it, Jesus replied, "Because of your unbelief; for assuredly, I say to you, if you have faith as a mustard seed, you will say to this mountain, 'Move from here to there,' and it will move; and nothing will be impossible for you" (Matthew 17:20-21 NKJV).

The mustard seed was the smallest known seed during those times and it is still one of the smallest today. Now there are different types of mustard seeds, but they are all very, very tiny. The smallest of them is about the size of a spec of pepper and could easily go unnoticed. Luckily for us, the little guy packs a lot more punch than you can see. A mustard tree can grow to be twenty feet tall, with its use being even greater! Your faith in your purpose may look small when it is next to your doubts and fears, but when it matures it will tower over it all.

Another thing that we must acknowledge is the process that we must go through when planting a seed. When you plant it, it disappears as it goes into the soil. You must water it and let it have light as you continuously put work in something that you cannot see. You do not know if your efforts are in vain because you cannot see the seed you planted. In time you will see it sprout up. Its roots will dig deep as the trunk and branches reach for the sky in counter motion to find more and more nutrients to help it blossom to its full potential. Once it reaches that point, you can finally reap the harvest and live within its benefits, *but there is more*.

This tree that you can use to feed you and others is also there for you to use to *exceed* its current potential by giving you even *more* seeds to plant *more* trees to have *more* during your time of harvest. So there will be a time when you doubt because you cannot see what you have planted and do not know what the future holds. Of course society will doubt you because all they will see at first is you putting in countless hours and investing a ton of effort into what they perceive as dirt. Your superiors will *definitely* doubt you because they have seen others miss the mark time and time again because they quit before it is time to harvest. You must have faith in the seed you have planted so society can join you once it sprouts from the ground. Your superiors will believe you when they are capable of seeing the results.

Dealing with No, Yes and Maybe

Doubt is a very nasty thing. It likes to come at you when you are weakest and will always raise its head before you make any positive life-altering decision. Just like anything else, ignoring doubt takes lots and lots of practice. You have to always make "no, yes and maybe" into "definitely." Take advice from kids learning to talk. When a child learns their first few words, all they want to do is use that word "no" for *everything* even when they do not really mean it.

You have to always make "no, yes and maybe" into "definitely."

Instead of saying "no" to everything, I want you to say "yes." If they say "no" to your proposition, just tell yourself they said "yes." If your friends are laughing at you and think you are crazy, just say yes anyway. If you do not think you can do this, just say, "Yes, I can!" Run around and say "yes" to anyone that doubts you and put a big smile on your face when you do it. If you *really* want to creep people out, say "yes" to them when they say "no" in your face. If they do not say "yes" right then, they will sooner or later. They may not know it, but your drive and persistence knows for sure that you can do it.

In the world of fitness, there is a belief that it takes four weeks for you to notice a difference, eight weeks for your family and friends to notice, and twelve weeks for the world to see the difference in you. For us, it is four weeks for us, eight weeks for society, and twelve weeks for our superiors to notice the difference in us. Remember, this is not a race, but a marathon. You are a boxer, a race horse, and a world-class, undefeated, champion. Do not stop until everyone's mouth is ajar because they cannot believe that you actually did it!

Doubt is a form of fear and fear is defeated by courage. It is okay to be afraid, but it is not okay to give into it. Combat your doubts with action and do not look back.

Faith Counters Doubt

Faith is something that we put into everything. You put faith in the car or the home you may be sitting in right now. There is faith in those people that designed and manufactured it. There is faith in the product itself. It's faith that the fire and brimstone does not fall from the sky at this very moment or some catastrophic natural disaster does not choose to show up at your doorstep. And there's faith that your loved ones are safe right now.

Facing & Confronting Doubts

We have to put our faith in everything and everyone surrounding us because we cannot be certain of a moment or individual.

You could be paranoid and think that the world is evil and everyone is trying to get you, live your life with your back against the wall, and with your eyes always open. Or you can choose to believe that all things turn out for good because they truly do. For every action there is an equal and opposite reaction. There is a purpose to everything. You may not know why as of yet, but you must put your trust in it until it manifests. So why not just put trust in your purpose and take the initiative.

> *May your choices reflect*
> *your hopes, not your fears.*
> *- Nelson Mandela*

Key Points

- Just remember that this is a fight that you can and must win.
- Their doubts mean nothing to you because you control your future now and you will not let anything get in the way of it.
- You have to always make "no, yes and maybe" into "definitely."
- Doubt is a form of fear and fear is defeated by courage. It is okay to be afraid, but it is not okay to give into it. Combat your doubts with action and do not look back.
- We have to put our faith in everything and everyone surrounding us because we cannot be certain of a moment or individual.

Digging Deeper

Take the time to go through this brief interactive section as you dig deeper into who you really are and what you are capable of doing especially in this area of dealing with doubt. Check each one off as you complete it.

- ☐ Circle your purpose with prayers and hopes as you take it from 2-D to 3-D with high levels of performance.
- ☐ Do not be square in your thinking because imagination is the catalyst for innovation.
- ☐ Triangulate your goals because there will *always* be another way for you to reach them by changing the plan, *not* the goal.
- ☐ Dig deep into your purpose as you stay obtuse to let loose of your never ending potential (like pi because 3.14 is the *very* simplified version).
- ☐ Always look for parallels to make this life make sense.
- ☐ Graph out a plan, pin point your coordinates, and rise to the occasion as you run towards your goals because failing to prepare is how you prepare to fail.
- ☐ Know your angles and find ways for your goals to intersect with the goals of others because it is by giving that we receive.

Chapter 11

Excuses

We have agreed that whatever doubts we had thus far are meaningless and only there to prevent us from engaging in our purpose and, in the very near future, exceed in our potential. The notion that you cannot is either absent or obsolete as you mentally progress towards achieving your purpose. But there is another adversary hiding in the midst. This one says that you will not as opposed to cannot. The sole purpose of this enemy is to render you powerless and become a victim of life as opposed to you living it. It is something that many of us use daily and consider a response instead of a choice.

Statements like, "She made me do it" or "I had no choice" come into play. It is often encased with deceit and procrastination as it preserves your current lifestyle, all the while keeping you in the same place as before. We must realize that, when all is said and done, we always have a choice. No matter the circumstances, there is one thing that we can always control and that is our actions. Even if they do put a gun to your head, you can choose character and tell them to pull the trigger.

An excuse is a decision based on priorities and comfort.

This section deals with choices and making *calculated* decisions. Too often we give ourselves leeway by basing our actions on our circumstances. When our actions are situational and not purposeful, we allow excuses to come into play. An excuse is a decision based on priorities and comfort. Priorities are the important and urgent matters in our lives. Ranking our priorities, similar to our belief in growing, comes about due to happenstance. Many of us never take the time to determine what is most important to us, leading to a *first come, first serve* mentality. This allows the urgent matters to sidetrack us. Because we did not set our priorities, life chooses for us because we preferred our own comfort.

Comfort-ability comes from the things that are natural to us. The decisions we make that put us at ease for that given moment. It is during the fast-paced decision making and the lack of prioritizing that we make excuses for whatever it is we finally choose to do. We use it to feel better about our non-purposeful choices by claiming innocence as we are not at fault for actions derived from a stimulus. We respond to the actions of others so it is not our "fault." It is the escape route from actions we do not want to do or the reasoning for actions we do want to do.

"For every action, there is an equal and opposite reaction."

We all know Sir Isaac Newton's third law of motion (especially because I am always referencing it)

It is the basis of all things and continues to correctly define our universe. In the realm of choices, the same thing applies. For us, the action or task is there to cause our reaction or response. We need to dig deeper in order to be *proactive* instead of *reactive*. Our response to a task can be reactive because we choose to live a life of comfort. Whenever there is a task at hand, we are given the opportunity to make a conscious decision on its priority and our comfort. The choices we have are to be highly comfortable with our high priority, lowly comfortable in our high priority, lowly comfortable with our high priority, or highly comfortable with our low priority. As you can see in the model, each one has a general thought process to it, all leading to a decision that is either based on reaction/proaction and excuse/choice.

	LOW COMFORTABILITY	HIGH COMFORTABILITY
HIGH PRIORITY	Planning, Relationship Building Budgeting Earned Recreation	Stimulated Deadlines Relationship Maintenance Credit/Loans Escape Recreation
LOW PRIORITY	Last-Minute Decisions Dramatic Relationship J-I-T Money Too Much Recreation	Neglect Unfruitful Relationships Financial Destruction Non-Stop Recreation

The principle states that whenever we are given a task, we choose one of these four quadrants to be our mode of action. Let's look at a few examples to make it more relevant.

Task: Studying for an Exam

	LOW COMFORTABILITY	HIGH COMFORTABILITY
HIGH PRIORITY	Planning times to study Reading/working material daily Study Group-Professor Visits Writing your own study guide	Studying the week of Reading/working what is assigned Joining a study group Taking teacher's study guide
LOW PRIORITY	Studying the night before Reading the night before Finding a study group last minute Borrowing someone's studies guide	Not studying Partying the night before No study guide Maybe not showing up

Task: Being Healthy (Physically)

	LOW COMFORTABILITY	HIGH COMFORTABILITY
HIGH PRIORITY	Planning times to exercise Having a proper diet Grocery shopping and planning recipes Writing your own study guide	Being active when a friend invites you to Eating properly when others are around
LOW PRIORITY	Crash dieting Intense workouts that cannot last Eating properly sporadically	Never exercising Eating whatever you want, whenener you want

Task: Wedding Anniversary

	LOW COMFORTABILITY	HIGH COMFORTABILITY
HIGH PRIORITY	Thinking up ideas months in advance Paying attention to things she is interested in Blocking off dates with work (for you *and* her)	Doing the same thing as last year Asking her what you should get her
LOW PRIORITY	Day-of reservations Day-of gift purchase (if possible to buy earlier) Stereotypical gift(s)	Forgetting the anniversary Acting like it's not important

Each instance has a set of actions that we do depending on which quadrant the task lands in. The quadrants all have a purpose and not all of them are necessarily bad given the circumstances. What is necessary for us to acknowledge is how important it is to actually decide where our tasks land to avoid them succumbing to our natural response of comfort and non-prioritization.

Quadrant IV

I know many of you are thinking that this quadrant is by far the worst of the bunch. It is true high comfort and low priority almost always takes the word *action* out of the equation. Although you are not performing the task, the choice to not perform is just as important. For me, one thing that consistently lands in Quadrant IV is cleaning my office. You would think that a person that is so hell-bent on organizing their life and decisions would be equally as OCD when it comes to the cleanliness of their personal space, but I am not. From the mountains of books, magazine articles, notepads, music scores, and anything else, you would think I was trying to have a competition with Albert Einstein to see whose desk could be the messiest.

My struggle with a tidy bedroom has more to do with the fact that I do not struggle with it at all. I neglect it because it really is not that important to me (although every mother reading this is having a heart attack). I travel so much that I do not spend that much time in it so it does not bother me. I know exactly where everything is and my room is my room so it does not affect anyone else. Things tend to get lost when I actually choose to clean it (honestly). I am more comfortable with it the way it is, and I do not consider a place where I rarely reside and where no one else resides a priority.

In other cases, when the task should be considered a higher priority, we just drop the ball. In that case, high comfort-ability and low priority is synonymous to the word *lazy*. Now, if you asked my mother why I do not keep my bedroom clean she would say because I am lazy. Quadrant IV is about as lazy as you can get because you choose to just ignore the task at hand. When you ignore the task at hand, it leads to the very thing we are trying to avoid, which are excuses. What you can expect out of Quadrant IV is a lot of losses, grief, and disheartenment because the more things you consider low in priority and the more you care about your comfort, the more selfish and reactive with excuses you become. In spite of the reasons you may place behind them, things in Quadrant IV, by default, are not high in priority. They may have their right to be placed there, but you must be sure they should be placed there as opposed to letting them just fall into the category. So yes, playing video games and going to the club ought to be *placed* in this category instead of *allowing* studying for an exam and making those cold calls.

If an action is to be placed in this category, the best way to assure its completion without you having to complete it is by delegating. A friend of mine is the connoisseur of delegating. Being a very successful businessman with multiple companies to run, he is not going to be the one to clean his room either. He intentionally puts this (and other tasks) in this category and delegates them. When you understand that something has to be done, but also understand that it cannot be of any priority and/or discomfort to you because it could hinder your overall performance in your purpose, you must go out and seek assistance in the matter. If you are one to have that mentality and understand its importance, you are definitely flirting with high performance and a life of significance.

Quadrant II

The quadrant most people between the ages of fourteen and twenty-five live in is Quadrant II. Procrastination and scrambling is practiced in this quadrant. Everything piles up and seems to come at us all at once. This lifestyle originates (for students at least) from exams and papers landing within the same week, along with galas and award ceremonies and anything else distinct to semesters and seasons. Doing everything last minute and constantly being in a rush is somewhat exhilarating, but also very tiresome. The mentality is to just get it done, but not to have it done to the best of our abilities.

Things are taken care of to avoid conflict and because we would be more uncomfortable if we fail to do the task. "I do this to avoid that" is essentially the mentality; that codependence mentality. So we study a few nights before the final to avoid failing the course. Purchasing the item on credit is to avoid spending our money now and taking a "sick day" is to avoid losing our cool and threatening our co-workers. We act now to prevent the possible negative reaction later, which still makes us reactive because our initiative is based on an outside variable. Excuses prevent a negative response that could possibly happen or to proactively enjoy what is currently happening in our lives.

Looking back on the example of studying for a final exam, the reason we have to cram the last few nights before is because we chose not to plan ahead for the exam. The date for the exam was set months ago, but we chose to hang out with friends or live in the current moment of high comfort-ability, making the high priority task to be worked on later to avoid a future moment of low comfort-ability. The decision was made time and time again weeks before the exam, but a day or two before the exam becomes high priority.

Quadrant III

Quadrant IV does not believe in responsibility and Quadrant II states that I will take up the responsibility to avoid a conflict of interest for future comfort-ability. Quadrant III is the bubble that either keeps things more towards Quadrant II and responsibility or will burst into Quadrant IV where there is no responsibility. Quadrant III puts an effort in a task for the sake of saying it has been done. We do not want to be in a position where the task has not been completed, but we do not want to break a sweat while doing it either. This is that "momma made me be here" notion. After kicking and screaming along with other forms of resistance, you finally fold and engage in what is usually seen as someone else's issue. It demands some form of attention from you because someone else requires it of you. For example, when looking at the wedding anniversary, you plan the dinner and purchase the gift at the very last minute because your wife sees the anniversary as a priority. Her priority becomes your priority. The mentality is you are doing them a favor. "She is lucky I even got the gift" is the thought that will come to mind.

The excuses come to save our skin and to avoid the reality that the only reason we chose to accept the task is because it was someone *else's* priority. It would be more uncomfortable in the future to tell our wife we do not really care about the anniversary, so we choose the latter by being uncomfortable now to prevent being uncomfortable (or dead) later as well. Honesty is something that has lost its step in today's society as half-truths and versions of the truth seem to be enough for all of us. But "truth is singular. Its versions are mistruths." Some may say it is necessary to hide the truth sometimes in order to save a situation or relationship. I say that it is necessary to make purposeful choices to avoid the situation entirely.

Quadrant I

When you are proactive and purposeful, your results will be progressive and plentiful.

Finally! The quadrant we have all been waiting for. Some people may call this the paranoid quadrant or the over-the-edge quadrant, but that is okay because thinking that means that it is something that most are not used to. Einstein said that insanity is "doing the same thing over and over again and expecting different results" so the more crazy they say you are the better you will be because when your actions are different, your results are different.

More relevant to us is when you are proactive and purposeful, your results will be progressive and plentiful.

Quadrant I is the fort with walls that are wide enough to have chariots ride on as the best archers in all the land restlessly watch for the enemy (excuses) day and night. It goes beyond retaining and maintaining by constantly thinking ahead and doing more by preparing for tasks before they even show up. This concept came to me while reading Dave Ramsey's *The Total Money Makeover*. Ramsey talks about how to not only get out of debt, but how to prepare for the worst, financially. He suggests having separate accounts so if there is a job loss or car trouble you are covered, all the while investing for retirement and future situations such as your kid's college tuition. When I was reading it I thought to myself, "Why not do this kind of thing in every aspect of our lives?" So I made it a mission in my personal life to do this as much as I possibly can.

One great example for me is my relationship status. Although I am single, I know I want to get married and have a family someday. In knowing this, I already have started planning for it because one of the things I want to see at my garden party are kids that never wanted for the necessities of life, but still have stern discipline and drive. I want to sit next to a woman that has become more beautiful each day we have been together due to me proactively striving to exceed our potential in love. I have already started thinking about ways I want to raise my children, different ways to celebrate anniversaries and birthdays, and how I will budget my finances so my kids can have the best education. Or, better yet, have them excel in their own potential so they can be awarded with scholarships that render my current budgeting obsolete. By keeping it in the back of my mind, if an idea comes up that sparks my interest, I write it down because I want to make sure that my future family have the best.

Talk about planning ahead! It does not make sense to wait to plan a fiftieth birthday party when your spouse is forty-nine and half. There is no reason why your project should keep you up the night before it is due when you were given a syllabus in the beginning of the semester with its due date. If you know you want to eat healthier and not depend on eating out, then take a night out of the week to cook for the upcoming one. If your manager expects a quarterly report then why not at least start an outline or pinpoint the key moments of the months leading up to it while it is still fresh in your memory. Taking care of the things that you can take care of in advance frees up your time and energy for other possibilities.

The general idea is thinking ahead because the reason for being a person that operates in Quadrant I can be summed up in one word: *growth*.

If you ever bought a flower for your home, you will notice how it begins to lean towards a window or door that reveals the sun. Its purpose in doing that is so it can get all that stuff flowers need from the sun to grow. Growth does not just happen. We either are forced to grow by life or we force ourselves to do it.

Exceeding your potential means your growth is intentional and you act intentionally by making decisions proactively. What happens to us in our daily lives is that we too often say "yes" to things when we really want to say "no" and that leads to our mediocre response to the tasks at hand. We say "yes" to avoid someone else telling us "no" or anything else negative, hence Quadrants III and II respectively. If we say "yes" and put it in Quadrant I, then we must be capable of putting things into Quadrant IV by saying "no" as well because we want each task to be done with excellence.

Working hard on what you do may not prepare you for every task, but it prepares you to work as hard as you possibly can for every task. That is why the preparation concept in Quadrant I is so important. So how do we get to Quadrant I?

Agree to Disagree with Yourself

What seemed to be another evening on the road with a friend turned into a memory that will now last a lifetime. We were talking about my book writing, his semester that would soon come to an end, relationships, and everything else that young men to talk about in the car. My friend's birthday was just around the corner, so I wanted to know what he was going to do for it. The man showered me with every sob story possible as he referred to midterms, papers, extracurricular activities, and responsibilities. I even think he tried to pull the "it is not that important to me" card.

Being the good friend (and often manipulator) that I am, I broke down the scenario with him. We had about a month before he could claim that he had lived another year, so I explained everything that he needed to do.

1 - Take sections of the midterms and start studying now.
2 - Make an outline for the paper and find a free weekend to write it, leading to nothing more than an edit when it was due.
3 - Take care of your responsibilities now so you do not have to deal with them then.
4 - Extracurricular activities can be put in the category of "no" because extra implies not necessary.

I saw in his eyes that he recognized how absurd his attempt to give me excuses was, so after a moment of silence I said, "Go ahead and agree to disagree with yourself, because the only person you are trying to lie to at this moment is yourself."

He looked at me, sighed, and asked, "You are going to put that in your book, right?"

The first step in avoiding excuses is denying yourself the luxury of lying both to yourself and others. The truth is something that many of us avoid because we do not know how people will react to reality. Due to the fact that we want to refrain from hurting feelings or making someone feel bad, we tell them part of the truth or cover it up with a lie. Remember, our response to a task does not come from that specific moment, but a compilation of decisions we have already made. So although we may now have to miss a family dinner because we have a presentation at the office, that presentation, more times than not, did not just come up the day before.

If we are honest with ourselves and the people around us, our negligence is usually the reason we make excuses for everything else. If we are proactive and a Quadrant I person, all of the things that are unnecessary go to Quadrant IV because we have made a conscious decision to tell people the truth. In reference to the family dinner, we only miss it because we made more decisions based on comfort as opposed to priority, not due to a presentation we knew of weeks ago.

Remember an excuse is nothing more than a decision based on priorities and comfort-ability. If you knew that family dinner would collide with a task then the decision to prolong your preparation on the basis of your high comfort is also the decision to make family dinner a low priority. When you chip away your reasons for making a decision on any task, it teeters between your comfort and your priorities.

Secondly, we avoid excuses and live in Quadrant I by pre-stating our priorities. If your family is more important than your job, but your occupation is still important, going out of your way to do the research and presentation earlier, working a bit harder, or even asking if the presentation date could be at an earlier or later date is something that will come to mind. Many may think that it is impossible to live by such concrete standards in such a competitive society, but there are examples all across the globe that beg to differ.

When I was in high school, a brother and sister lost their father in the middle of a semester. Their family is of a particular Jewish descent that I cannot recall and very devoted in their faith. When the father passed, there were specific things that they could and could not do in order to pay homage. They were out of school for some time in order to practice their mourning process. When they returned they did all that they could to make up their work, and did well that semester in spite of losing their father. They were capable of doing that because they had their priorities in order.

Their faith and their family were more important than education, but they still deemed their education important so they did what was necessary to make it all happen, in spite of their discomfort.

When you set your standards in stone, some may not respond to it as well as my alma mater did, but that is okay. You will feel much better standing up for priorities than you would letting them be dismantled by someone or something. In doing the latter, you become a part of their priority instead of your own. Just ask the owner of Chic-Fil-A who still refuses to have his stores open on Sunday in spite of popular opinions and financial advice.

Knowing our priorities, sticking to them, and being honest are ways to avoid excuses. Another way to avoid them is by being sacrificial. This is probably the toughest to uphold out of all of them. It is also the one that will not only change your life the most, but change the lives of those around you as well. When we are specifically referring to sacrifices and excuses, its focus is on putting others before you. When we lie, we do it more for our comfort than anything because we do not want to have to deal with the response from the truth. When we take up tasks and work on them with mediocrity, it is because we want relationships to stay the same. What happens when we do that though is we are not giving up anything. Although it may seem we are because we think about the way they feel or we are doing them a favor, we are not. This will become obvious when we come to them when we are in need and say we did them that "favor" so now they are obligated to do one for us.

Selflessness in Quadrant I are always asking the question, "Would I want someone to do that for or to me?" If you do not want to be lied to then you need to sacrifice your desire to avoid confrontation and tell the truth. If you would not want people to give you 50 percent of themselves when asked a favor, then you should not agree to give it to them to have a favor in your pocket to call upon them for because "they owe you". If you would not want your wife to be on her phone when you two are having a romantic dinner then you should not be on yours when she is asking you a question in the family room. Be consistent and precise in your sacrifice. Make it second nature and never hold it over someone's head.

It is in the sacrifice that we grow and become better people. Our potential's foundation is our character. Nothing is ever solved when we give people what they deserve. It is in our giving of grace and mercy that creates change. And it is in giving that we receive.

Key Points

- Growth does not just happen. We either are forced to grow or we force ourselves to do it.
- Exceeding your potential means your growth is intentional and you act intentionally by making decisions proactively.
- Working hard on what you do may not prepare you for every task, but it prepares you to work as hard as you possibly can for every task.
- If we are honest with ourselves and the people around us, our negligence is usually the reason we make excuses for everything else.
- Remember, an excuse is nothing more than a decision based on priorities and comfort-ability.
- It is in the sacrifice that we grow and become better people.

Digging Deeper

What is necessary for us to acknowledge is how important it is to actually decide where our tasks land to avoid them succumbing to our natural response of comfort and non-prioritization. Begin by completing these definitions of each of the Quadrants discussed in this chapter.

Quadrant IV does not believe in _____.

Quadrant II states that I will take up the responsibility to _____ *a* _____ *of interest for future comfort-ability.*

Quadrant III puts an effort in a task for the sake of saying _____. *We do not want to be in a position where the task has not been completed, but we do not want to break a sweat while doing it either. This is that "momma* _____ *me be here" notion.*

Quadrant I goes beyond retaining and maintaining by constantly _____ *and doing more by* _____ *for tasks before they even show up. The general idea is thinking ahead because the reason for being a person that operates in Quadrant I can be summed up in one word:*_____.

> *Which quadrant best describes where you are right now in your lifestyle?*
>
> *Which quadrant do you really want to be in?*
>
> *What do you need to do to achieve that goal?*

Know your priorities, stick to them, be honest, and be sacrificial to avoid excuses.

List or review your priorities and post them where you can see them every morning.

Look at your list at the end of the day and evaluate how you did in sticking to them.

Be honest with yourself and make the necessary changes.

Chapter 12

The Threshold

It is important to shift our mental behavior in order to successfully engage ourselves and work on exceeding our potential with consistent high performance activities.

The road less traveled has made us independent by focusing on our own character and relying on what we determine to be of high priority in our lives in order to successfully act on the tasks set before us. As we travel deeper into the rabbit's hole, we must dig deeper into the understanding of ourselves. We need to understand how important our existence is in reference to the purpose that God has designed for us in order to connect to the world and impact it in a positive way.

Jumping into your purpose before shifting the way you think will make it too big and your character too immature to uphold the tasks ahead. Not taking the leap at all means you still look at your purpose and yourself as being too small and irrelevant to be something that can help you and society grow. Similar to Alice and her wonderland, if you drink from the bottle, you reduce in size and continue to live the life current as wealth in your purpose continues to evade your grips. If you eat the cake, you physically grow exponentially, but not in character so your foundation cannot withstand the pressure. The balance amongst the two is a hard one to grasp, but it is something that you must discover as you go deeper into the rabbit's hole and discover the wonders in *your* land.

The Threshold

What is most important is not whether or not you make the right/wrong decision(s), but if you are learning from them in order to change your mental behavior and understanding of growth.

When my father first came up with the idea of starting his own church, everything about the dream seemed implausible. The first seemingly ridiculous notion that came about was how he did not only believe he would pastor his own church, but that it would be one that already had its own pastor! Every time we passed that old church on the corner, he would tell all of us, "I am going to pastor that church one day."

My entire family would cackle because my father was very involved in our current place of worship, an evangelist that would travel near and far to preach, and a doctor that had the secular career of being one of the heads of a very well-known hospital in New Jersey. This was huge during this time period as my father played the lead physician role in the middle of the anthrax pandemic. This made his plate look a little too full for anything else.

Regardless of the facts, when I would be in the car with him once a week, he would talk about pastoring that church on the corner of Old York Road. It was not until two or three years after his purpose came knocking on his door that he was capable of attaining it when the opportunity opened up. What my father taught me throughout his journey to become a pastor with his own congregation is something we can all learn from as we break the threshold.

Seven Threshold Breakers

Here are the seven breakers that I recommend for taking the next step deeper into your purpose and potential.

Having Faith in the Call: That subtle tug on your heart and mind has been placed there for a reason. The purpose designed for your life can only be achieved by you and you alone. It is not a coincidence that the vision rang your bell and requires your attention. Each person has their own specific contact number that no one else can replicate. These digits are a representation of the "what, how, and why" that create your purpose and form the potential within you that must be exceeded in order to be a person of significance.

When I got the call to go to college, I wanted nothing to do with it. The university I attended was not even on my list until the deadline week for applications. After visiting that Christian liberal arts school in Tennessee, I knew there was a purpose for me there, although I did not know what. Transitioning from sports to music, North to South, and large to small school in less than a couple weeks psyched me and my college advisor out, but that was because we could not see what the future held.

Not until I attended the school and joined one of the greatest a cappella groups in America did I understand how I would apply my life's purpose. *Voices of Lee* lost all of their bass singers the a couple weeks before my first semester at Lee University, so there was a void that only I could fill. *Voices of Lee* travels every weekend and upholds a rigorous schedule during the school year, but I was prepared because I went to one of the best college preparatory high schools in the nation that had classes six days (yes, six) a week as opposed to the typical five, along with the number of extracurricular activities I was a part of during my time there.

I never wanted to take out student loans to pay tuition and I had no idea how I would reach that goal and go to a private university, but I received an academic scholarship due to my standardized test scores and *Voices of Lee* also had a scholarship program that I did not even know of until after I made it in the group. Both *Voices* and I had very specific needs that were met solely because I had faith in the small, still voice that was telling me to apply to Lee University at the last minute. That same voice is the reason I decided to write this book and will be the same voice that will propel me into the next phase(s) in my life. It is also the same voice that will propel you in yours.

Referring back to the spiritual aspect of our lives, there is another realm that defies time and space. It is in that atmosphere where we are connected to all living things from the past, present, and future. It is in that portion of us, where the calls in our lives and the lives of others coincide and help things fall into place. It never makes sense in the beginning, but that is why faith is necessary. You never really know who is on the other end of the call until you answer it anyway.

Respect the Process: The schemes created in today's society to fabricate growth always lead to quick results and even quicker returns to previous habits after prematurely pulling the seed we have planted to grow. We have the world's most amazing super computer sitting right between our ears, but we choose to treat it like the steam engine. Initially, it is going to take quite some time to reprogram your brain so it can properly attune to your purpose and discover the first steps of exceeding potential. After the thousands of neurons intertwine and grow to connect the different lobes in your brain's cortex, the process will be easier and growth will happen much faster. However, you must respect the first few stages that take the most time and effort even though, at that point, there are very few visual results.

Just imagine you decided to start your first garden by planting the seed of your choice. It takes days upon weeks for any visual sign of growth as it hides underneath the Earth. Do you dig up the ground to make sure the seed you have planted is still there? If you do, you must restart the entire process all over again in order to get a sprout, making the duration even longer than before. Yet we constantly like to check out the pace when it is not time for us to evaluate what has happened in our growth. It is not until there is a sprout that you can see that the evolution of what has been planted and honed is apparent. Once above ground, advancement quickens and the progression can possibly be expedited as slowly, but surely, the plant gets used to growing.

I remember when one of my nieces was just a few months old. Keeping her quiet and getting her to sleep through an entire night was a victory in her maturation in the beginning because she was only a baby. After turning one, it seemed that she went from crawling to walking overnight. Words began to form in her mouth and her cognition became a fun and enjoyable treat to witness as things made more sense to her. Although we had to be careful because opening doors and changing the television channel was something she somewhat understood from watching us do it, her brain just sucked up every bit of information possible. She would not be where she was at the age of two, unless we first taught her how to do the little things necessary for her body and mind to grow correctly. It was slow at first, but things are moving much faster now and will continue to move faster simply because we took our time with her in the beginning.

The process can be frustrating, especially at first, as the brain, body, and spirit connect within, making us a more suitable candidate for reaching and exceeding our potential. We may not see how our character is expanding to prepare to uphold the weight of our purpose on its shoulders, but it is in having faith in the call and respecting the time it takes to answer the call where we discover who we really are and what we can truly be capable of.

Be Comfortable with being Uncomfortable: One of my least favorite superheroes of all time back in my childhood was actually the staple of all comics. The hero of heroes, Superman, was a character I loathed due to his ridiculous set of skills and unrealistic strengths. It was not until I actually read the comics (because I'm a nerd so accept it) that I began to learn how difficult it was for the Man of Steel to become the Man of Steel. In spite of the fact that his body was always impervious to most elements in the universe, his powers did not just come to him overnight. Shooting lasers from his eyes and even flight is something that we all know Clark Kent to have, but he had to train his body and mind in order to get the strength necessary to reach them. It took getting to a certain peak in a super power that he tried to see how much further he could go. This was how he went from uncontrollably shooting rays of lights from his retina to controlling it so he could do something as fine and precise as brain surgery. Superman first learned how to jump high and far prior to his achieving his mach speed capabilities in the sky. The only reason this super Boy Scout reached these points in his abilities and beyond was because he got comfortable with one thing: growing.

Curiosity and faith in what could happen lead Clark to constantly put effort outside of his comfort zone in order to reach another level in his strengths and, at first, weaknesses. The oxymoron, get comfortable with being uncomfortable, is one known throughout the ages, but not one that most of us implicate. Most of us would rather be comfortable than attempt to do anything that actually requires any form of effort. If that was not the case then more of us would be focused on exceeding our potential. That is why shifting our mental behavior is vital when it is time to break the threshold into physical behavior.

Your mind is what tells your body what to do, that is why you need to take the time to first program the way you think before you program the way you act.

Commit to Priorities: Which one do you want more, the accomplishment of your priorities or the accomplishment of your comfort-ability? That is the outstanding question that separates your dreams from becoming your reality. When high priorities in your purpose connect to the high priorities in your life, productivity is a flowing river that never ceases to amaze. The issue with that is never the difficulty of these priorities, but our commitment to them. Movies and novels always put the protagonist in an impossible situation that they overcome because they practically have no other choice.

In the film, *Taken*, it is clear what the priorities of Liam Neeson's character are. A man that has very little connections and nothing more than a general location and a very faint accent finds a way to rescue his daughter from the hands of human traffickers in a matter of days. The scenario was very black and white: Rescue your daughter or never see her again. He could have put himself in a victimized position by reporting to the authorities and waiting in hope of the accomplishment of his goal. Instead, he took matters into his own hands because he knew that his desperation would be his inspiration to conquer a father's greatest fear. There was nothing that would come between him and his purpose, which is why he successfully reached his daughter and saved her. (Well, that and it was a movie.)

When you commit to a priority, it cannot be something that is attempted haphazardly.

A friend of mine used to joke about this when referring to his dating life. He told me that the way he goes about getting a girl on a date is by telling himself yes, although she may say no. He would say, "I can see her mouth shape into a yes as her vocal chords vibrate with sound. Just because she said no today, does not mean she will not say yes tomorrow." The fact that he envisioned these unfortunate ladies saying yes was enough for him to continuously go after them, in spite of a no. It was all because he was committed.

Committing to your priorities makes everything black and white. The bottom line is you either achieve your goals or you do not. For us who focus on exceeding our potential, you either achieve your goals or you learn from your failures. You may have missed the mark, but do not miss the lesson you can take from that moment so you have a better shot at it tomorrow. If life comes at you with a big and resounding no, just remember that you have seen it say yes in your mind, so have faith in your purpose and stay committed to what is now your priority.

Remember, Big Brother is Always Watching: The biggest reason we usually cut ourselves some slack whenever we put effort

The Threshold

in anything is because the only judge that could possibly see us throughout the process is ourselves. Our actions behind closed doors and in the dark involves us alone, so we often take advantage of that and choose comfort over priority.

The fact of the matter is you are right to believe there is only one person who can rightfully judge your actions and thoughts, but that person is not the *current* you. Whenever I think about my fullest potential, I can actually picture a bigger and better me that is capable of beating me in any challenge brought up. More importantly (for me at least), I have the upmost faith that "full potential me" could lay the smack down on my candy assets (if you catch my drift). Full potential me, or big brother, is *always* watching. He is so determined to be a real person that he keeps me up working into the wee-hours in the morning, ignoring sleep and food in order to successfully reach the next level in my potential.

Big Brother is always talking my ear off, motivating me and reminding me that a person's character is tested when there is not anyone around to see the results.

When I first decided to go out on my own after I quit my job, I had nothing. My goals were so far in the future that I did not even know where to start at first, but that changed after a while. Once I got my bearings, I would go around and act as if I was the person I hoped to be. I wanted to be a speaker and writer that traveled across the globe, helping people exceed their potential so that is the way I acted. Every time a project would come about, I acted as if it was the most important one, because if I did not then Big Brother would dropkick me in the throat for dampening his future character. A global Phenom has to be capable of communicating with different cultures so I started reading anthropology and sociology books.

A true entrepreneur knows how to dress to impress, so I would walk around my house in a button-down shirt, slacks, and dress shoes. At first my family thought I was crazy when I walked around the house, fully dressed at eight o'clock in the morning, but they appreciate it now. They and everyone else that knows me understand how important it is to look your best. My friends and I almost always wear our suit and tie like Justin Timberlake whenever we have a celebration and spend time together. I cannot even remember the last time I have seen a pair of sweatpants on me or anyone who hangs out with me unless we are going to the gym. That is because we all established our Big Brother.

Big Brother can be a big pain, but he only wants what is best for you because it is what is best for him/her. Believing that he is watching will keep you in line when you see a corner you could possibly cut. It will help your mental behavior as you constantly remind yourself how important it is to keep your character symmetrical to what will be your physical behavior. Besides, Big Brother, full-potential you, also has a big brother, and he exceeds full-potential you. He is not ready to play yet, but he is just waiting to jump on board.

Keep in Touch with Big Daddy: Understanding the importance of interdependence is one thing, but comprehending it is something that neither of us can truly fathom. This is why keeping in touch with Big Daddy is vital at this turning point in life. Whatever your spiritual beliefs are, that deity is what connects your potential and purpose to the world. I know I am not smart enough to plan every single detail of my future that involves the sea of people in society and including their own personal potential and purpose. The only way I can keep the course, especially at a time such as the growth of my mental behavior where I cannot see *anything*, is by staying in tune with God. My daily devotions help conduct the moments I will have within those given twenty-four hours and is the only way I can possibly have faith in the call.

This next leap that puts you into action and creates a physical behavior that can coincide with the mental one continuously growing, will try to bring you back to a place of doubt and excuses. Having faith in your current self would be an absurd thing to do because current-you will not be the one holding the baton at the end of the marathon. By looking that far in the distance of life can be frightening and, more than likely, confusing because there are so many steps in between. You have to find someone that can see the macros *and* micros simultaneously. That individual that can help you shift the scope respectively and assure your success. That is held within the spiritual realm by God.

The only way to know how to get to your why is by speaking to the person that created it just for you in the first place, and that is Big Daddy—God.

Move…Act…Don't Procrastinate: If you take the time to look at the careers of the rich and famous, you will quickly see how much of a roller coaster their lives were in the beginning of their course. From the average millionaire dealing with and overcoming at least one bankruptcy before hitting the seven-figure mark, to great talent like Fred Astaire and Walt Disney being told they were everything *but* great, and even individuals such as Paul Mitchell and Halle Berry being homeless, all took the leap over the threshold in spite of their positions. For some, their economic status may not have been compatible to their potential. Others, their mental behavior may not have been up to par with the physical so they went back a few steps.

From bad to worse to worst, every story has a ***defining moment*** where they have to make a choice to either let their dream remain up in the sky or lasso a rope around it and drag it on down to grasp it in the palm of their hands. The idea is to take action no matter what the circumstances may be simply due to the fact that the worst thing to ever come out of "failing" is the lesson learned. Actual failure only happens we choose to stop making the attempt. Breaking the threshold and putting our thoughts into action is something many tend to avoid and is the reason many of us are so miserable. We know our purpose and might even have the capacity to overcome those bad mental habits, but we still cannot take that leap of faith.

Before my father got the building that he stated would be his future church all those years ago, he took a leap of faith after reaching the mental behavior necessary for physical action by starting a Bible Study group in our community. There were weeks during that time when my family did not have a church home so Sundays were just us in the living room having devotions. After a couple months of that, my dad had an opportunity to rent out the community center and let that be where New Hope Church of God met on Sunday mornings. He would always set up at least 100 chairs in the building, in spite of the fact that our "church" might have had twenty people (at most). He believed that there would be a time that we would no longer be able to fit in that place. He knew his purpose and believed in his potential within it, so every week I would help him put out one hundred chairs.

It is amazing, looking back now, how ridiculous *we were* for thinking how crazy he was for doing that (among other things). Needless to say, we did outgrow that community center and he did pastor that church on the corner. In less than ten years, he went from just that one church to three with over six hundred members in the congregation. In a day and age where religion is being bombarded with negativity, especially the Christian faith, such growth is unlikely. My father took action and exceeded his potential time and time again. He has a knack for speaking things into existence after first working out his mental behavior. His next level of potential and dreams is one that seems crazy to my family yet again, but now we know it will happen. The biggest thing he did, though, happened ten years ago when he put his thoughts into action.

This next section discusses the shift in our physical behavior and how we can take what we officially deem as possible and of high priority and put it into physical, tangible action. The threshold is not one you walk through, but jump into. The idea is to take the leap of faith and figure out how to *build* your wings on the way down.

Just remember that though the process is uncomfortable, it is necessary as you prepare to meet your priorities and build your character. Big Brother will make sure you keep going so just pray to God you can reach and exceed your potential before you reach and exceed the ground!

Key Points

- It is important to shift our mental behavior in order to successfully engage ourselves and work on exceeding our potential with consistent high performance activities.
- It is in having faith in the call and respecting the time it takes to answer the call where we discover who we really are and what we can truly be capable of.
- Your mind is what tells your body what to do, that is why you need to take the time to first program the way you think before you program the way you act.
- When you commit to a priority, it cannot be something that is attempted haphazardly.
- Big Brother is always talking my ear off, motivating me and reminding me that a person's character is tested when there is not anyone around to see the results.
- The only way to know how to get to your potential is by speaking to the person that created it just for you in the first place, and that is Big Daddy God.
- Breaking the threshold and putting our thoughts into action is something many tend to avoid and is the reason why many of us are so miserable.

Digging Deeper

Here are the seven threshold breakers that I recommend for taking the next step deeper into your purpose and potential. Check them off as you complete them in your own life.

p **Have Faith in the Call:** That subtle tug on your heart and mind has been placed there for a reason. Have faith that the one who gave it to you has also given you what you need to accomplish it.

p **Respect the Process:** The process is one that can be frustrating, especially at first, as the brain, body, and spirit connect within and without themselves, making us a more suitable candidate for reaching and exceeding our potential.

p **Be Comfortable with being Uncomfortable:** The oxymoron, get comfortable with being uncomfortable, is one known throughout the ages, but not one that most of us implicate. Time to implicate it in your own life.

p **Commit to Priorities:** Which one do you want more, the accomplishment of your priorities or the accomplishment of your comfort-ability? That is the outstanding question that separates your dreams from becoming reality. If life comes at you with a big and resounding no, just remember that you have seen it say yes in your mind, so have faith in your purpose and stay committed to what is now your priority.

p **Remember, Big Brother is Always Watching:** The biggest reason we usually cut ourselves some slack whenever we put effort in anything is because the only judge that could possibly see us throughout the process is ourselves. The fact of the matter is you are right to believe there is only one person who can rightfully judge your actions and thoughts, but that person is not the *current* you. What is your Big Brother challenging you to do today?

p **Keep in Touch with Big Daddy:** The only way to know how to get to your potential is by speaking to the person that created it just for you in the first place, and that is Big Daddy God.

p **Move:** By now you know your purpose and know you have the capacity to overcome those bad mental habits, but have you taken that leap of faith? The idea is to take action, no matter what the circumstances. Ready, set, go!

Chapter 13

Engagement

Up until this point, we have been dealing with the things that prevent us from being active in our purpose by rewiring our mental state and focusing on exceeding our potential. Discovering that doubts and excuses are devices used to implement idleness in our purpose has lead us toward the mental behavior shifts to make us capable of advocating proactivity in our physical behavior. Physical behavior is the "umph" in triumph as we put our thoughts into action by strategically going through a system that will assure our prosperity. This system catapults us to the next level in order to reach our goals and exceed our potential. We do this by finally being engaged in our purpose and initiating change in our lives and in the lives of others as well.

Will You Marry Me?

Since I am not married yet, I can only imagine what it would be like to "pop the question." Doubt and excuses would definitely be in any guy's mind when he asks for the blessing of the parent(s), goes out to look for a ring, tries to figure out when and where he is going to ask the question, etc. When you finally do everything you can do, then you have to lay it all down and put it in the hands of someone else in a single moment. Now *that is* scary.

In essence, engaging yourself to your purpose is almost identical. To be engaged in your purpose is to occupy your actions with it. Thoughts are transitioning from the mind into the body as your efforts reflect your purpose. You may not be fully confident in what is to come, but you are further ahead now than before so it is time to walk the talk you have been speaking to yourself thus far. You have overcome your doubts and the doubts of others and have decided to overlook any excuses that may come about in order to take initiative. It is time to put yourself out there for the world to see and let them make the decision, just like asking someone to marry you.

Once the decision is made, we enter engagement and go along the arc of influence. The arc of influence is an idea I heard by my mentor Jonathan Sprinkles. It is the transcendence into our purpose by exceeding our physical behavior as we create the habits necessary for greatness.

The arc is split into four separate categories that each and every one of us are actually living in whether we are conscious of it or not.

1. Survival - The push towards being engaged in our purpose
2. Stability - Purpose and personal life in one accord
3. Success - The union of strong mental and physical behavior
4. Significance - The secrets of High Performance

The ongoing process of the arc of influence is what distinguishes those that strive to be more by choice rather than by force.

Each category has a very important role in your purpose and goals, but the pinnacle is a place of significance. It is in the significant position that you have the most control of your future. It is understanding how vitally important how you do *what you do* and knowing *who you are* in the world that you live in and the world to come. It is in significance that proactivity and interdependence coincide to create the person that you aspire to be. The significance position is the area of performance at the highest level. So let's strap ourselves in and climb to the mountaintop starting with the first category—survival.

Survival Mode:
Moving Away from This Place

"This is stupid." "I feel stupid." "Why am I here?" "What in the world am I doing?" "How in the world did I get here?" "I don't know what's happening?"

If you have said any of the above phrases then you know *exactly* what I mean when I say that survival mode is the place that you want to get away from **as soon as possible!** Reaching this position in and of itself is a miracle because most people never make an attempt to follow their dreams, let alone put as much thought into it as you have thus far. Remember desperation always leads to the inspiration of the great things this world has offered.

Darwin's Theory says the strongest do not survive, they adapt. The only way to adapt is to be in a place that you are not used to and in a position that you are uncomfortable with. Here is where your priorities to meet your goals outweigh your comfort, putting you in Quadrant I in the Excuse Diagram. Your mentality shifts so your actions shift as well. More importantly, the reason *why* you shift is what leads you to this current position and will lead you out of it as well.

The reasons for actually engaging may vary but it is important that we understand what they are:

1. *Either Or:* If you look at all of the rags to riches stories out there, you will notice that all of them had one of two choices. They *either* starved to death *or* they found a way to make their dream(s) work. Walt Disney was notorious for always putting everything he had into his goals, almost bankrupting him and his company numerous times, but it was in that position that the two choices became only one. The "no other choice, but to. . ." makes your

purpose the only way out, and puts you into a position that brings action.

2. *Sick and tired of being sick and tired:* Another form of desperation that trades idleness for engagement is when you have taken the last straw. When you decide that you can no longer continue on the path you have been going on, you put yourself in a place of desperation because if you do not, life would be meaningless. The continuation of life as it is must no longer be. Your mind tells you that enough is enough so it is only a matter of time before your actions tell the same tale.

3. *What is the worst that can happen:* Every once in a while, the decision to act comes from a calculated decision as opposed to emotion. The decision to let go and let God is entirely cerebral, which makes it the most difficult one to use as your reason for engagement. It is either the worst has happened so the only way to go is up or the opportunities of good outweigh the bad so an attempt is in order.

Beam me up, Scotty!

It is good to understand why you are engaged, but it does not help you understand how to get out of survival mode. The fact of the matter is you are still nervous beyond measure because you do not really know what you are doing, and that is okay. We are fortunate to not have the technology to disassemble and reassemble our atoms from one place to the next like Captain Kirk and the crew of the Enterprise because it means that we have to make our own way out.

This is not the road everyone goes on or even the road less traveled. This is the road never traveled because the only person that can see its path is you! There are no shortcuts. You cannot parachute or paraglide or para-anything your way onto this rare piece of soil. You would not even have known where this remote course was unless you had chosen the path you are on. The next few steps along the trail are hidden by even more vegetation than the Amazon rainforest. There is nothing fun nor entertaining about this next part because there is nothing but grunt work along the way. With machete in hand, it is time to push your way through the forest in order to survive survival mode. By doing nothing more than acting in your purpose day and night to get a little ahead of the curve, you will make it. So prepare to wipe the sweat off your brow to get through survival mode. Declare right now Gloria Gaynor and say, "I will survive!"

I Will Survive

The first thing you must know about surviving survival mode is that you **will** actually survive. I know it feels like the apocalypse and your heart is preparing to flat line (if it does not burst out your chest first), but that is okay. Actually, that is more than okay. If you do not feel that way then you need to go back and make the dreams bigger and the goals more preposterous because your actions must be relevant to the potential you desire to exceed. The only way to do such things is by having a purpose that sounds impractical. It is natural to be frantic and slightly crazed at the moment because that is the physical response to a place of desperation. It is supposed to be scary. It is supposed to be challenging.

You already took one big step by discovering your purpose, another big one by changing your mental behavior, and a huge leap into the abyss by acting on it.

The first time I stepped on stage with the *Voices of Lee*, I was praying that sweat was the only thing running down my legs because I was so nervous. For most people, doing *anything* in front of an audience is scary, let alone singing with a group of people that will literally crucify you if you do anything but *their* standard best. I mean learning close to thirty songs from *memory* (including choreography) with an acapella group that does eight-part harmony is tough enough. Having to learn it all and be ready to perform it in two-weeks as I took close to *twenty* credits the *first* semester of my college career would be considered about impossible for most people.

The great thing about digging deep is that you and I are **not** in the "most" category. It is our potential, our destiny, and our goals that make it possible even if everyone around us believes otherwise. Not to mention that due to the fact that we are exceeding our potential, the feats that we must overcome are designed for us not only to face, but to overcome. Proving them (and yourself) wrong is a difficult task, but remember that the word impossible is relative to only one thing: time. This next section is designed for you to be encouraged as you push through survival. Read it everyday as a reminder that what must happen at this point, *will* happen.

It is in your persistence and perseverance that causes fiction to become fact.

1. *Say It Wit' Yo' Chest!* To continue with my freshman year with Voices, when you are given the biggest 3-ringed binder ever made and are told to memorize all that is within it in two weeks, the *last* thing you need to do is doubt yourself. The first thing you have to do is accept the challenge and *know* that it is going to be done because you are persistent and perseverant. That has to be your mindset from the get go!

One of the reasons a lot of us do not make it through survival mode is because we give ourselves the luxury to think we have a choice. We do not have a choice. **The only way to get out of survival mode is to get through it, and get through it strong!** We have to see that the door we walked through to get this far has officially disappeared. Big Brother took the liberty of making that door behind us into a cinder-block wall that has booby traps inside of its booby traps so that the only way out is by going through the next door toward our destiny.

In *Seriously Funny*, Kevin Hart talks about his uncle who had been in jail (just bare with me here). After getting out and determined to make it in the world, he would always say the phrase, "Say It Wit Yo Chest!" to people whenever they would speak to him about what they wanted to do. In other words, "Say it like you mean it." When that obstacle is in front of you, the only way to get through it is wholeheartedly. You cannot do the hokey-pokey and gradually get your entire body into the circle. You have to just jump on in there and turn yourself about (because that's what it's all about). You have to have a sense of boldness that supersedes anything that you have ever experienced.

How is that possible? It is possible because your solution is already within you and you already have the tools needed to overcome whatever lies ahead because it was designed *for you*. In essence, you have already *won*. The only thing that prevents this science fiction from being science fact is the time it takes for you to walk (or strut if you have swag) on into victory. You do that by knowing you have got what it takes. So say it *wit yo chest*!

2. Stage 5 Clinger: Since you are doing this wholeheartedly, you are now going to be considered a "stage 5 clinger." A stage 5 clinger is a very, very, *very* obsessive person. So obsessive in fact that they can (and more than likely will) be viewed as crazy. Those two weeks I had to prepare those songs, I do not think I went anywhere without my ten-pound binder. (It was literally that heavy. I weighed it). I used every bit of time I could find to read, listen, and practice. If I was not in a practice room clonking on the piano to hear the notes, I was listening to previous recordings of the group. If I was not listening to the recordings, I was looking at the sheet music. If I was not looking at the sheet music, I was looking at the words to the songs, and so on. I would listen to the music in the car, in class (which I apologize for), and even in my sleep, hoping that my subconscious could get me just a little bit closer to my goal.

I would look at the music while walking to class (which nearly got me killed a couple times), when I would go out with friends, and when I ate my meals. I would see music notes in my dreams

I worked on it so much, but that was what it took for me to get through survival mode.

Michelangelo said, "The greater danger for most of us lies not in setting our aim too high and falling short; but in setting our aim too low, and achieving our mark."

When you aim high, you have no choice but to do some pretty radical things. It is always easier to divert back to where you have been as opposed to reaching a place you have never reached. Obsession is necessary because it is what gives you the capacity to persevere.

3. 22-Iso: In football, there is a running play that "isolates" the linebacker. The isolation basically means you *could* block him, but you do not *have to* block him. The lineman or full back goes right by him and acts as if he does not exist. That is what you have to do as well when you are going through survival. I did not watch television during those two weeks. I did not go to my dorm in between classes. I did not sit around and chat with friends. I did not even make it to my bed sometimes because I had a friend with a piano in his room so I laid on the floor in the commons area if I needed a nap. I isolated myself so I could work on and achieve what I needed to do to get through survival mode.

Isolating the necessities of life is what gets you to be fully engaged in your purpose. In this consumer age, we tend to confuse wants and needs and that is why we put ourselves in a predicament that continuously gives us less than what we truly desire. Most would say that you do not give 100 percent or put your all into life. The question is not if we are giving 100 percent, it is where that 100 percent is going. We all have 100 percent, but if you put 10 percent into television, 20 percent in playing video games and 40 percent of it in sleeping then you just wasted most of your efforts.

We will speak more about implementing 100 percent even when you are enjoying times of recreation, but there comes a point when your actions are so in sync with your character that it does not matter what is going on, you are always doing something relative to your purpose and exceeding in your potential.

We have to get through survival mode by isolating all of our actions toward our purpose in order to make it to the next point.

4. Repetition, Repetition, Repetition: You know when you have come out of survival mode when you are *comfortable* with what you are doing. I did learn all of those songs within the two-week time period I had, but I was still shaking in my boots when I got on stage for the first time. I knew I was where I had to be, but I was not necessarily where I *wanted* to be. Reaching the end of your goal(s) will be something that is odd and uncomfortable at first.

Many of us never actually achieve anything we set for ourselves, let alone something that is so much bigger than ourselves. We must get acclimated to this new environment in order to successfully get through survival mode. The only way to make it to the platform that will keep you away from survival mode hereafter is by doing it over and over again.

Repetition is how you form the habits that are required for physical behavior.

The more you act in your purpose, the more your body adjusts so the actions become second-nature. Once you are stable in your purpose, you can transition into stability mode where you balance life and purpose.

Key Points

- The ongoing process of the arc of influence is what distinguishes those that strive to be more by choice rather than by force.
- Survival: The push towards actively being engaged in your purpose.

- You already took one big step by discovering your purpose, another big one by changing your mental behavior, and a huge leap into the abyss by acting on it.
- It is in your persistence and perseverance that fiction becomes fact.
- Michelangelo said, "The greater danger for most of us lies not in setting our aim too high and falling short; but in setting our aim too low, and achieving our mark."
- We have to get through survival mode by isolating all of our actions toward our purpose in order to make it to the next point.
- Repetition is how you form the habits that are required for physical behavior.

Digging Deeper

It is important to understand the reason for actually engaging in the required physical activity needed to successfully achieve your life's purpose. Which one has moved you into action? Explain your personal situation.

1. *Either Or:* The "no other choice, but to. . ." makes your purpose the only way out, and puts you into a position that brings action.
2. *Sick and tired of being sick and tired:* Your mind tells you that enough is enough so it is only a matter of time before your actions tell the same tale.
3. *What is the worst that can happen:* Either the worst has happened so the only way to go is up or the worst is trolled by the best, so an attempt is in order.

It is in your persistence and perseverance that what most consider impossible becomes fact in your life.

1. **Accept the challenge:** *What is the only thing that prevents this science fiction from being science fact in your life?* _____

_____

Do you know you have got what it takes? _____
Then say it *wit yo chest*!

2. **Define a Stage 5 Clinger:** _____
_____ *is necessary because it is what gives you the capacity to* _____ .

3. **Isolation Stage:** *We all have 100 percent to give, where is your 100 percent going?*

List the things you did today and see how much time you spent on each one.

Evaluate where you spent your 100 percent. Where do you need to make changes?

The more you act in your purpose, the more your body adjusts so the actions become _____ . What are you going to do to achieve this in your own life?

Chapter 14

Stability and Success

"Congratulations, you are the winner of your hit show, Survivor!"...now what?

You have gone through the shadows of death (along with the fiery furnace) and the gnashing of teeth by pushing your way through every obstacle and trial that life could throw at you. You have your foundation in your craft, but now you must mesh it with your life. It is time to swing the pendulum towards the center so you can enjoy your life as you live it within your purpose.

Stability is when you go from you being the influencee to the influencer.

Similar to the order of doubts, your capabilities first begin with you being the influencer of your life. After learning all the music by consuming my life with my new found purpose, I had to find a way to have the best of both worlds. Basically, I had to take my purpose, my why, and let it be used in other "hows.".

Going back to our purpose, the titles and positions we discovered in "the how" more than likely have its own tasks that are of high priority. After getting settled in your purpose at this specific moment in your life, we must bond our other responsibilities along with it. We will go back to the long-term goals we have set in terms of family, education, influence, and experience, within the parameters of our titles, and then schedule ourselves to make sure everything gets done and we meet our intentions.

We go about this by first designating the titles we will be holding up for the week ahead. After acknowledging these positions, we write down the goals we want to meet for that given week along those lines in order to properly spread out the tasks that need to be done. For example, if there is a book that you want to read this given week, you may want to carve out an hour or two each day to read it. If one of your family goals is to take the wife out on a date monthly, maybe this week is lighter than the others so you can give yourself a window for dinner and a movie (and perhaps more).

As the owner of your own company, you may need to address departments and check-in with employees in terms of your influence goals, so you can plan that accordingly this week as well. Perhaps one part of your goals is physical so you need to educate yourself in this area in order to be healthier, so outlining a couple hours, three to five days this week, will help you achieve them. Those things that are high in priority are set throughout the week as such, or can be scheduled as specific engagements each day. Planning your life this way gives you more space to respond to unexpected events or a better opportunity to rearrange your itinerary if needed.

Transitioning from survival to stability is a way to live a more fluid and paced life that is better handled. Survival mode is pedal to the metal as we try to sustain our purpose, but stability is letting off the gas a little so we can grow, but at in a more viable stride. It is in these moments that we can form the habits necessary for our physical behavior to be consistent and productive *long term* as we look at each task and place them in the box or boxes suitable for their importance and our comfort-ability. Our short-term and long term goals need to be clear so we can strategically put the things important in any given week between priorities and engagements., As we do, we set ourselves up for a more positive and purpose-driven life. It is in living this way we can reach the next stop in this arc of influence, and that is success.

Success

So you have survived the first phase of your purpose and reached a place of stability along the way by making it your foundation to balance the rest of your life upon. The next point of influence is success, where you influence not only your own life, but also the lives of those close to you. The mode of success is more of a time to reap and appreciate what has happened thus far. Up until this point, you have been setting both mental and physical behaviors that are designed to build the character for your purpose. Along the way, you have continued to grow and constantly meet your goals and create new ones, hence exceeding your potential.

Now, after creating such a great name for yourself, it is important to influence others and help them reach the same capacity. Although you never stop learning, you are now capable of being a teacher to your family and friends by being a person that exceeds their potential. Similar to your own personal growth, the shift will not happen overnight and will more than likely not happen because they have specifically asked for your assistance. It is time to plant seeds in the gardens of others in hope for a better tomorrow for us all.

Without a shout of a doubt, everyone wants to be considered successful at some point in their life. For us, the qualifications for success is a life that can impact others in any of the four goal setting categories we made when defining the "what" in our purpose and in the previous chapter involving stability. As stated earlier, the process in the arc of influence first deals with yourself forming a foundation in your purpose and then letting it be the base of your life. The next step is the current one where you can use what you have built to work with society or people you usually interact with daily.

We reach this position because our physical and mental behaviors are so in tact and in tune with where we want to be, that others want to have the same type of success in their lives.

It is an unspoken challenge within your loved ones and colleagues that will eventually take you all to another place in your potential. The reason why I find this notion so important is because one thing that is vital when you are trying to achieve goals are the people around you. No one gets to the top by themselves, no matter what many may try to believe or portray. Each of us have a core group that has helped us along the way, some without even knowing it. They have all played a huge role in our being successful within our purpose and are one of the many reasons for why we wanted to be at this place. Let's go through how we get our closest counterparts to reach the same point.

Physical Behavior is Designed to be Seen

Success leaves a lot of clues along the way. Although your trail will be different than others because it is supposed to be, the process to get through it has the same form of structure. When acting on your purpose, it is important to allow the things that should be visible be so for numerous reasons. For starters, letting your goals be known in your circle keeps you accountable. Just the fact that you told another person what you desire to do helps you exponentially. Even if the individual(s) don't do anything, you subconsciously acknowledge the fact that someone else knows what you plan to do. Due to the fact that your mental behavior is keeping up with the physical, your success will be witnessed and desired by others.

Be an Exemplifier, not a Director

Let's face it, the people we love can be our toughest critics. After knowing us for years, we have taught them a very specific way to treat us. Our past habits taught them the way we used to behave and that is all they know. The change will be suspicious to them, even at this point of success, but they know that shift is now fixated into your life. The problem is not knowing this to be true, it is knowing that it can be true for them as well. When you reach the point of success, you risk having the Messiah complex as you attempt to save everyone you hold close by telling them what they should and should not be doing in order to get there. Annoyance will be more of the response than acceptance when trying to do that.

We cannot direct people into a place of success.

Doing so actually defeats the purpose because they will be more dependent on you to tell them what to do as opposed to them discovering the answers within themselves through spiritual guidance and their connection to all things. The greatest teachers tell you where to look at, but not what to look for. Although it takes more to go this route, it is the only way to assure their own independence. The only way we can help our family and friends is by being an example. Our behavior in both realms is one that is natural to us at this point so it is not an actual task when doing so, but it does demand our attention in order to help others reach another level.

Feel Free to Bring Up the Challenge

When I decided to write this book, one of the first things I did was challenge my father to do the same. My father has been talking about writing a book for only God knows how long, and yet I was capable of getting my first one under my belt before he probably even wrote the first paragraph (I say lovingly to *still* challenge him). Being a huge sports fan makes me quite the competitive person.

It is natural for many of us to step up to any challenge that comes our way. Our desire to reach for something outside of our grasps is the very basis of exceeding potential, but it is even more enjoyable when there is someone on your side striving to do the same exact thing.

Bringing up the challenge is beneficial to you because there is someone on your coat tail throughout the process.

It is also beneficial because it can strengthen the relationship(s) you are in, which should be one of our goals anyway.

Be Patient and Remember How Far You Have Come

Nothing used to be more frustrating than watching my father try and "tutor" my sister when she was in grade school. As she struggled with math and science, my father tried to help her in those subjects he was most comfortable with. But, the more he tried to help her, the less he was actually capable of doing so because he expected my sister to just pick it up and understand it after one quick explanation. His current knowledge in the subjects blinded him from remembering how it was for him in the past. Having a doctorate in anything is about as far as you can go and here he is trying to revert back to the days of multiplication and the periodic table; nearly impossible to do, right?

When we reach the success level, we must remember how much we have grown thus far, especially when we are interacting with others who have yet to reach this place in their lives. Their ignorance is not intentional and we must understand that the process to gain the knowledge about themselves will take time.

If we are truly willing to help, then we must go at their pace and recall how much effort we took to have the character to reach this point in our lives. It is only then can we be successful in our purpose *and* successful in helping others do the same.

The world considers success as someone that has wealth and power, and that is partially true. However, those natural rewards are not the most important part of success. How you implement them is.

If wealth and power are used only for your personal gain, then its success is pointless to have, at least in terms of living a life of purpose.

Supporting someone to escape a life of dependency is worth more than anything money can buy. It is a true definition of power because we are helping individuals have power and control in the most important thing: *Themselves*. Acting at this capacity is what we will use to springboard into the next place in this arc of influence, which is significance.

Significance is a position that very few reach because there is another factor to the equation. It is one that we have yet to truly discuss, though it is the most important aspect for high performance. Are you ready to be significant in this world?

Key Points

- Stability is when you go from being the influencee to the influencer.
- We reach the position of success because our physical and mental behaviors are so intact and in tune with where we want to be, that others want to have the same type of success in their lives.
- We cannot direct people into a place of success.
- If wealth and power are used only for personal gain, then success is pointless, at least in terms of living a life of purpose.

Dig Deeper

Each of us have a core group that has helped us along the way, some without even knowing it. Fill in the blanks as you reinforce the main ways this may have happened in your life to help you reach the success realm. Think of how you can now use these principles to help others reach their success realm.

Physical Behavior is Designed to be Seen:

Due to the fact that your mental behavior is keeping up with the physical, your success will be _____ and _____ by others.

Be an Exemplifier, not a Director

The greatest teachers tell us _____ to look, but not _____ to look for.

Although it takes more to go this route, it is the only way to assure their own _____.

The only way we can help our family and friends is by being an _____.

Feel Free to Bring Up the Challenge

Bringing up the _____ is _____ because there is someone on our coat tail throughout the process

Be Patient and Remember How Far You have Come

If we are truly willing to help, we must go at their _____ and recall how much _____ we took to have the character to reach this point in our lives.

Chapter 15

Performance: Significance

Well, ladies and gentlemen, we are finally here! It is time to get down to the "nitty gritty" (as Nacho Libre would say) and get ourselves to the big boy/girl table. When we go to family celebrations and things of that nature, there is always a kid's table, the teenager's table, the "grown-up table" (with all of the random family members that people do not pay attention to), and then the big boy table where those family members that made it big hang out with grandma and grandpa. This is that table with all of the fine china and nice fancy chairs, along with the food actually being on the table instead of having to go get it on the buffet line. That is this table!

When we are in significant performance mode integrity and consistency define our character and our destiny.

On Like Donkey Kong

People of significance have many things in common. One that is very specific for all of them is their high performance level in correlation to the significant point on our arc of influence. Performance is defined as executing or acting on a specific work or task, but we shall dig deeper than that as we move towards fulfilling our purpose in the most significant way. In order to make the huge

Performance: Significance

leap from success to significance, we must go beyond what most people do. The average person usually executes on the specific tasks at hand, but that is the bare minimum. Although some may celebrate the fact that they are "just doing their job", we want to take it to the next level. Our desire to be purposeful in all that we do implies that we want to transition from our actions being *what we do* to them being *who we are*.

We do not just act on our work, we *become* our work. Our purpose in life should not be what we *do*, but *who we are*.

The idea is we are high performers that dominate our specific work or tasks. This position that is upheld by the strongest of characters, created by the mental and physical behaviors we have formed, are designed to be in correlation to the habits we consistently implement in our purpose. But how does that happen? Remember how I said that there is a surprise in this section? Well, the surprise is another behavior. This behavior may be last, but it is certainly not the least of the three. In all actuality, it is the most important one to have as we move to exceed our potential because it is in this behavior we separate ourselves from the crowd and define our significance. It is how we establish our interdependence. Here is how we learn the interaction between our purpose and the community by strategically enforcing some really cool factions that most would not even think of, let alone act on.

Ladies and gentlemen, I give you the behavior of *spirituality*! Now before you grab incense and sing kumbaya, let's discuss what spiritual behavior is. Spiritual behavior consists of the ins and outs that keep this entanglement within our world constant and significant for our purpose and wealth. Physical behavior was *acting or working out* our purpose and mental behavior was *working within* our purpose. Spiritual behavior is how we work *on* our purpose. It is the stuff *behind* the stuff. Spiritual behavior (in conjunction with the other two) is similar to any movie or television show. Mental behavior is the directors, producers and writers that come up with the script and plot. They are there *working within* the storyline by jumping into their own imagination to make something magnificent before anyone even has an idea to what the future holds. Physical behavior is the actors that bring what has been written to life by *acting out* on the mental behavior. Spiritual behavior is the group of people that nobody really knows, but is the core group that makes everything into the magical motion picture(s) we enjoy. These people are the reason why the end credits last ten minutes. They are the ones *working on* connecting both the idea(s) and the action(s) to allow what has been created come to life for the world. *The stuff behind the stuff.* As we plan some really neat activities that give us the opportunity to open our chances to be more significant each and every day, we start the process that allows our purpose to define us. If something is to define us then it is in us. When something is in us then there is no such thing as clocking in and out, as "vacation time", and/or taking a day off in the figurative sense.

Now do not get me wrong, there will be time to relax and enjoy the finer things in life, but that is also something we will touch on in this section because if you are as serious about your purpose as I am then it is necessary to schedule that in. When you are in significant performance mode, integrity and consistency defines your character and destiny, as what you do becomes who you are.

Spiritual behavior is how we work *on* our purpose by planning activities that give us the opportunity to be more significant each and every day as we allow our purpose to define us.

There are seven things to take out of in significant performance and are things that you should strive to do *every single day*. One of the reasons a lot of us do not reach our goals is because we simply give up too early. We make *changes*, but we never make *shifts*. If we make *changes*, then we can always change back, like our hair color or a career. If we make a *shift*, like in a labyrinth, the route we used to get where we are is no longer there. It is through this paradigm shift that we create things that last a lifetime. It is in the habits we create within our spiritual behavior that our significant performance becomes our lifestyle.

Here is the breakdown for performance:

Preparation
Elevation
Reverberation
Following Up
Opening Up
Relaxation
Maintaining

The Spiritual Seven.

These dukes of our spiritual behavior are going to blow us away! The workload will be more than anticipated and things will be tougher in the beginning, but it is never easy to have something live inside of you (just ask any mother). It is even harder to have that something inside you have the strength to be so impactful that it reaches out and affects the lives of others (just ask any *seasoned* mother). But when we are significant, we do not just sit at the big boy table at family Thanksgiving; no, no, no. People of significance get to sit at the big boy table *everywhere* they go. They sit at the head table at a non-profit event, the Executive Committee table during a company meeting, and any other table imaginable that holds those that create change. Ready to step into this realm of high performance and significance?

Starting with S.E.L.F.

> *Love your neighbor as yourself.*
> (Mark 12:31)

We have all heard the phrases "love your neighbor as yourself" and "do unto others as you would have them do unto you." These statements are definitely important to implement every day in our life, but most of us fail to do them correctly. We mess up in the "as yourself" part. See, I believe that we must love ourselves *before* we can love anyone else. Our society would think it selfish and rude to put ourselves first and that is true if you are doing it in the narcissistic sense, but in a giving sense, it is exactly what we are told to do. The word "as" means to the same degree or extent. So how could we successfully express love for another if we cannot properly express it to ourselves?

You will always do a poor job representing love for another if you do not strongly love yourself. This is something that should be applied, but how does it relate to significance? As a singer, one of the most important things to do before any performance is to warm-up. Actually, one of the most important things to do in the entertaining industry in general, from sports to acting, is warm-up. In doing so, you are preparing the muscles so they can gradually warm up to their peak performance. It is just too dangerous to exude a ton of stress on the body abruptly and it would be counterproductive to your goals at that given moment.

As productive individuals, we *should* warm-up every day *before* our day, but we tend to put it to the side and then wonder why our careers and relationships seem to be getting worse rather than better. Well, it is because you are just jumping into your day, every day, without a proper warm-up! Most of us carve out enough time to shave and shower so we can hop in the car and scurry into the workplace just before our boss yells at us for being tardy. That is *not* preparing yourself for the day. Remember your first day of school or work? You woke up early enough to get yourself ready. If you are truly an overachiever, you might have set your clothes out the night before. Your morning actually included some time alone to get yourself in the right mood mentally. You actually got there early. You actually had breakfast! Remember how much better you felt when you walked through those doors? When you start your day by properly preparing yourself, you open up all of your behavioral muscles so they can perform at their fullest potential. As humans, there are three core parts of our being that need this proper daily warm up. Those three are *mental, physical, and spiritual*. I like to call them the "Big 3." There is an illustration that I learned from the great Stephen Covey that really brings the idea home.

I attended a seminar once when the instructor was lecturing on time. At one point, he said, "Okay, it's time for a quiz." He reached under the table and pulled out a wide-mouth gallon jar. He set it on the table next to a platter with some fist-sized rocks on it.

"How many of these rocks do you think we can get in the jar?" he asked.

After we made our guess, he said, "Okay, let's find out."

He set one rock in the jar. . .then another. . .then another. I don't remember how many he got in, but he got the jar full.

Then he asked, "Is that jar full?"

Everybody looked at the rocks and said, "Yes."

Then he said, "Ahhh." He reached under the table and pulled out a bucket of gravel. Then he dumped some gravel in and shook the jar and the gravel went in all the little spaces left by the big rocks.

Then he grinned and said once more, "Is the jar full?"

By this time we were on to him.

"Probably not," we said.

"Good!" he replied.

And he reached under the table and brought out a bucket of sand. He started dumping the sand in and it went in all the little spaces left by the rocks and the gravel.

Once more he looked at us and said, "Is the jar full?"

"No!" we all roared.

He said, "Good!" and he grabbed a pitcher of water and began to pour it in.

Then he said, "Well, what's the point?"

Somebody said, "Well, there are gaps, and if you really work at it, you can always fit more into your life."

"No," he said, "that's not the point. The point is this: If you hadn't put these big rocks in first, would you ever have gotten any of them in?"

Mental, physical, and spiritual. The Big 3.

The Big 3 should be the *first* things you do on any given day to assure your success in all of the little details throughout any given day. You are the center of your world. If you are not at 100 percent performance level when you *start* your day, then how do you expect the rest of your day to be? That is why it is important to start with your S.E.L.F.

Start with S.E.L.F.

S.E.L.F. stands for Solitude, Exercise, Luminosity, and Faith. These things represent your mind, body, and spirit which are your mental, physical, and spiritual self. These are the very things that encompass your existence. Preparing these three things, in conjunction with the isolation process we discussed earlier, is how you begin to be significant in your day-to-day living. It is necessary to make sure that your "me time" truly focuses on nothing else but you in order to serve the world around you properly.

Remember that luck is when preparation meets opportunity. The only way to make sure that you are always prepared for that opportune moment is by doing so before you have any encounters. Doing these things in the beginning of your day, every day, are the first steps to gaining significance in your life.

For high performance and significant individuals, every day is a purposeful one.

Solitude: In this age of constant motion and endless interaction, I am pretty sure the word silence is not even put in the dictionary anymore. In knowing this, it is important to make some time for yourself to do whatever it is necessary to be at your peak performance. Whenever you are getting ready to propose a big project or conduct some major deal, you usually want some time for yourself to get your stuff together.

Performance: Significance

For high performance and significant individuals, every day is a purposeful one and is deemed a major deal. So if you want to be a high performance individual, you must treat everyday as such by having your moment of silence.

What I tend to do is wake up a few hours before my first appointment for the day just to take care of *me*. In understanding how you would want to be treated, you can definitely do more for someone else.

Exercise: I know, I know. The last thing you want to think about when you wake up in the morning is being physically active in any way, shape or form. But, it is scientifically proven that exercise does wonders for the brain. From memory to stress reduction, the endorphins that are released along with the sweat being extracted from your pores when physically active makes exercise great for you, especially before your day truly begins. If something is that great for you then you are definitely loving yourself in order to love others. So what are the things we can do to wake up our bodies for the day?

A long walk	Resistance training	Stretching/Yoga	Bike Ride
Breathing exercises	Hiking	Swimming	Cardio

Logic: *We all know that leaders are readers and learners are earners, but if you make that be your thing to do at the end of the day then it will almost never get done. And let's be honest, none of us want to go back to our school days of falling asleep with the book either on us or us on it. We need to go ahead and put our educational goals at the beginning of your day because it assures their success as it wakens our mind. The great part about seeking intelligence in the beginning of the day is the endless possibilities. From concentrating on the task(s) for the day to plotting our future endeavors (especially the ones within our purpose), we can do a lot of things for the layers of neurons in the tissue inside of* *your skull when we start our day stimulating our brains. How do we find a way to we get our brains in gear for the day to come?*

Journaling	Reading	Studying work notes	Practice a language	Puzzle games
Play an instrument	Dream BIG dreams	Planning your day	Online brain exercises	

Faith: *Something that is always neglected Monday through Saturday is faith. Most of us just wait to get our dose when we go to whichever place of praise on those treasured days we call weekends (and even then it's a rarity). Although I am not specifically talking about any religion (or religion at all for that matter), the trinity between body, soul, and the world is something we take for granted. You can say what you want about religion, but we are all definitely connected and that is due to a Creator. It is important to acknowledge that before the day in order to love others as us bc this Higher Power loves us more than anything else in existence. How does one prep their spiritual behavior in the early morn?*

Meditate	Pray	Plan community service	Read faith-based literature
Listen to inspirational words/music	Study the laws of the universe		

Key Points

- When we are in significant performance mode, integrity and consistency define our character and our destiny.
- We do not just act on our work, we *become* our work. Our purpose in life should not be what we do, but *who we are*.
- Spiritual behavior is how we work *on* our purpose by planning activities that give us the opportunity to be more significant each and every day as we allow our purpose to define us.

- For high performance and significant individuals, every day is a purposeful one.

Dig Deeper

Physical behavior is working in your _____ _____.

Mental behavior is working within your _____.

Spiritual behavior is how you work on your purpose by planning _____ that give you the opportunity to be more _____ each and every day as you allow your purpose to _____ _____.

What does it mean to have your purpose define you? _____ _____

One of the reasons a lot of us do not reach our goals is because we simply give up too early. We make changes, but we never make shifts. What is the difference and why is it important to make shifts instead of changes? _____ _____

As humans, there are three core parts of our being that need this proper daily warm up. Those three are _____, _____, and _____.

The only way to make sure that we are always prepared for that opportune moment is by _____.

Doing these S.E.L.F. things in the beginning of your day, every day, are the first steps to gaining significance in your life and in the life others.

Solitude: *How are you going to make some time for yourself to do whatever it is necessary to be at your peak?*

Exercise: *So what are the things you can do to wake up your body for the day?*

Logic: *How are you going to get your brain in gear for the day?*

Faith: *How are you going to prep your spiritual behavior in the early morning?*

These four necessities will give us a head start for the tasks set before us on any given day. They make everything prosperous due to the fact that we are preparing ourselves for high performance. Starting with ourselves will show that there is more to a day than we think and there are a lot of positives we can appreciate by doing so.

Prioritizing: If there is one positive that you will definitely get when starting your day with S.E.L.F., prioritizing will always be on the top of the list. When you begin to wake up earlier in the morning to prepare for a day and *then* go about doing it, you learn what things matter to you *very quickly*. For me, personally, I tend to wake up around 4 or 5 in the morning (crazy, I know) to prepare for my day accordingly. It took me a while to get the habit of doing it, especially because I am definitely a night owl, but I have more accomplished by noon than most will have at the end of the day, mostly because I do not mess around with my time anymore. Things that come around last minute are almost immediately thrown into the low priority sector of excuses until I get the important things done first.

Create your standards/rules about anything that goes outside of your routine and stick to your guns. Family, friends, and coworkers *all* know to give me, *at the very least*, a couple days notice for any event they want me to show up to. They know to give me, *at the very least*, a few weeks' notice if I they need my assistance for an engagement. If they do not then I do not. If you let people put their plans into your life and rush to their aid, then you are on their agenda, not yours, You are also crippling them by constantly saving them from the mess they put themselves into. If you are *always* doing things for them last minute then that is what they will expect and they will be even more dependent on you than before. You might as well throw on a cape and put a mask over your head because you have officially taught them to rely on you to save the day. This is counterproductive not only in your growth, but in theirs as well! You teach people how to treat you so teach them properly.

Everyone may not want to conform to the new and proper way you should be treated, but that is okay. Your purpose in life is not to please everyone, but to exceed your potential and do more with what you have so you can leave that significant footprint in the ground that will last throughout the ages.

Set your goals and stay on track because if you don't then the world will continue to pass you by and you will continuously get the results that you *don't* want.

Accomplishment: *There is definitely a sense of accomplishment that you will have when you start with your S.E.L.F. every day because you are accomplishing something! Waking up a couple hours earlier than most people will lead to you getting so much more done in your day even before the day really starts. Your body craves whatever you put into it. If you are constantly accomplishing things that early in the day then you can expect yourself to do the same throughout the rest of it. Just try it and review your accomplishments at the end of the day. You will be amazed at how productive you have been, how much you have grown, and how much closer you are to success.*

"Success is not to be pursued; it is to be attracted by the person you become" and that person grows each day when you take the time to nurture your future, significant self.

Focus: *A friend of mine used to always ask me first thing when he saw me in the morning, "What are you looking into getting today?" I used to look at him like he was a few cards short of a full deck when he first addressed me this way, but then I got to thinking about it.*

The odds of us getting what we want are higher when we are focused on getting it.

If you are just focused on getting through a workday then that is all you will get. If you are focused on the date with the girl from communications then you will go through every possible conversation you will have with her throughout the *entire* day. (Trust me ladies, we over think those moments the same way you do. Do not let the macho man persona fool you.) If you are focused on having a successful day and doing something significant then that is exactly what you will achieve because you have locked your sights in on it. That time of solitude and goal setting is definitely where you focus and figure out what you are looking into getting each day.

Rest: *If you want to really talk about learning how to prioritize, your sleeping schedule will be priority #1 when you start taking care of your S.E.L.F. I learned how to go to bed at a decent hour so I could get the right amount of sleep necessary for the following day. Quality sleep is something most of us do not get because we like to put other things in front of it. But, when you are* **not** *living to have just enough to make it, you will quickly do more than get just enough sleep to make it through the next day. Turn off the television. Don't sleep with your phone by your bed. Avoid late nights with friends during the week. You will be* *surprised how more rested you feel when you start waking up a bit earlier and starting your day with S.E.L.F.*

The main thing to realize with all of this is that time is the *only* thing in life that you cannot get more of.

Once time is gone, it is gone. We may not all have the same amount of time in our lives, but we all have the same possibilities of investing the right things in the time we have. There is no Indian-giving when it comes to your time. If it was a bad investment then it is something you must make up and fix. When you start with yourS.E.L.F. each day from now on, you learn how to invest your time properly and have more assets than liabilities.

Evaluation

High performers understand the importance of creating opportunity for them to excel in their fields and exceed their expectations and the expectations of others. In order for one to do that, you must be capable of evaluating not only yourself and your situation, but the situations that are to come as well. The dictionary defines evaluation as the act of determining the value or the amount of someone or something. In order to do this, there must be two things one must gain knowledge of: where someone is/was and where someone desires to be. This system is created by combining the three aspects of life that we have been speaking of thus far (mental, physical, and spiritual) by creating goals, creating habits to meet these goals, and continuing the process to stack our results exponentially. Let us start with creating goals because it is when we work from the end that we get to the end.

Creating Goals

We briefly spoke about goals when we were defining our purpose and looking at the *What Bubble* which is the focus on the tasks we must accomplish to successfully excel in our purpose. We shall dig deeper (pun intended) with this topic in this section because goals laid before you are what help gauge your performance and since we want to be high performers. . .you get the gist.

1. Think RPG Big

I am pretty sure that we have established how big of a (cool) nerd I can be at times so just bare with me here. Role Playing Games or RPGs used to be one of my favorite games to play. (For those of you who do not know what that means then think World of Warcraft and no, I never played WoW.) One of the reasons why so many people can spend so much time playing these games is because of the vast opportunities laid out before you. As a gamer, you get to literally create the life you want to live. As long as you have the mind to dream it and the time to put the effort into it, your world in an RPG is essentially limitless. That mentality is the mindset necessary when creating goals. Think of this time as a fantasy realm where everything is at the palm of your able hands. What would you do? What goals would you want to accomplish? Get lost (with the pun also intended here) in your creativity and come up with some off the charts goals.

2. Speak in FPS

Since we are already here in the analogy of gaming, another focal point in creating goals is very similar to the world of First Person Shooters or FPS games. FPS have you, the gamer, *is the character*. Your eyes are in the first person narrative and everything you say and do is officially that person in the game; your goals should be the same. If you say, "I want to make a lot of money" then you will constantly create the effort, but never the outcome because your focus is on the *want*. If you state, "I have large sums of money", then your energy will go towards the production of this declaration as oppose to the possibility.

Another aspect to acknowledge is the importance of keeping everything present tense. Do not think that you want it; know that you already have it. Declaring what you have has more urgency to creating the person necessary to achieve the goal.

3. Be Specific

Goals are dreams with deadlines and, when appropriate, measurements. Instead of saying "I am debt free", say "I am debt free 365 days from now." Here again, having a time table creates a sense of urgency necessary for someone that is wanting to make a dream become a reality. To be even more specific, put a number for the subject (which is currently debt) as well. Now the goal sounds like, "I have attracted X amount to be debt free 365 days from now."

4. Be Positive

Another aspect of creating goals is assuring positivity. It is a lot easier to push towards as oppose to pull away from something. To continue with the previous example, if you say "I have a positive net worth of X 365 days from now," you are more likely to push towards that as oppose to pulling away from the latter.

5. Write & Speak

There is nothing worse than having goal(s) and then forgetting about them. There is a reason why judges have an evaluation sheet that they use to write down what they have discovered from the contestant. Our focus stays geared to the things we write down as oppose to the bustle in the world around us. And, when I say write, I legitimately mean ink and pad (and that does NOT mean iPad). Another thing to do is to read your goals out loud when you first wake in the morning and right before you go to bed. There is a spiritual power to speaking things into existence. When we hear who we are, that becomes the focal point throughout the entire day and what we dream to become when sleep at night. Reading your goals *every* day until completion will assist in creating them in the real world. God spoke everything into existence, right?

Creating Habits

We all know the importance of doing something consistently. The habits we create are what define who we are and will be the catalyst to exceed the goals we want to obtain. This is how the mental creation of the goals becomes a physical reality. There are three things to do to get to this place.

1. State who you are

Remember Big Brother? Well, this is where we will properly create him. Pick any one of your goals and make a description of what type of person someone must be in order to obtain them. Focus on general definitions similar to the example given. Make sure that you put all of the information in present tense and in first person just like your goals.

2. Acknowledge the habits you currently have

This next part will be the least amount of fun you will have throughout this entire book because it requires you to be brutally honest with yourself. The issue that many of us have when it comes to achieving our goals is not giving the proper amount of time necessary to achieve them. The first day of my accounting class back in college, my professor took someone's average day and split up how much time they put into each thing. From sleep to classes to the time it takes to travel, everything was calculated and split within the twenty-four hour window we all have on any given day. After all of this, she said that we all have 100% to give, but we tend to put that energy in the wrong place(s). Her challenge to us was to catalog each minute of each day for a week and to then go back and figure out how many hours are spent on each thing. As you can imagine, that next week when we were all in class, *no one* wanted to be used as an example. One of my friends (that she picked to use as the human sacrifice), spent about four to five hours playing video games. . .a day! Between *2K, Battlefield* and being too competitive to walk away from a winning streak, he would end up in the living room with his roommates doing this for a much longer time than he thought; not to mention the fact that a lot of the time he was eating or "doing homework", he was still in the room with everyone else playing video games so it still counted. Now, the part that really killed us (but mostly him) is how she calculated the time spent. X Hours divided by 168 hours (which is the amount of hours in a week) gave us the percentage of time spent on any given action. (Bare with me on the math here.) So this is what his time spent on video games looked like:

5 hours x 7 days = 35 hours per week
35 hours / 168 hours = 21% of the week

This college student spent more time playing video games than he spent on his occupation as a student. One out of every five hours a week, he would be playing video games. These numbers are staggering, but they are also necessary. When we take the time to catalog our time used or the amount of food eaten or the money spent for an entire week and then calculate the percentage, the shock will make us want to change our habits. This is when we make the exchange or the shift.

3. *The Shift*

As stated in creating goals, it is important to keep ourselves positive. After acknowledging our bad and good habits, it is time to make a shift in our daily routine so the good outweighs the bad with something I call the Goal Digger Shift Form.

Underneath the description of the person that you want to become, create a T-chart. One side will be the new habits that you want to start *and* the current good habits you want to dig deeper into. The other side will be the poor habits you want to stop. Now after writing these two lists, pick three to five healthy habits that you can trade for three to five unhealthy habits. Write down the healthy habits you want to expand on and *how* you will do so. It is important to actually apply these things in your daily routine because that is the only way to successfully become the person you need to be to obtain your goal. Now, for the next three weeks, implement these new healthy habits daily to create *The Shift* from the old unhealthy ones and voila, you have officially killed two birds with one stone. One poor habit has been destroyed and a good habit has taken its place just like that.

GOAL: I am 45 pounds lighter in 2016
Description of WHO I AM GOING TO BE
<ul><li>I wake up early to exercise for thirty minutes.</li><li>I only eat organic and non-processed food.</li><li>I take the stairs instead of the elevator.</li><li>I prep my meals the night before and pack them for the next day.</li><li>I eat every 3 to 4 hours and always have a meal prepared.</li><li>I go and do physical activities (biking, hiking, bowling, etc.) with my family once a week.</li><li>I always look at the menu before going to a restaurant and find a healthy meal.</li><li>I look for the healthier alternates and substitutes when applicable.</li><li>I am able to have one treat meal per week.</li></ul>

New and current good habits to dig DEEP into	Poor habits I am going to stop
<ul><li>Drinking at least one gallon of water daily</li><li>Standing at my desk instead of sitting</li><li>Finding a workout program</li><li>Going grocery shopping once a week</li><li>Carrying a healthy snack with me at all times</li><li>Getting 8 hours of sleep a night</li><li>Exercise for thirty minutes five days a week</li></ul>	<ul><li>Going to fast food restaurants</li><li>Eating after 8:00pm and having late nights out</li><li>Eating junk food</li><li>Drinking soda</li><li>Having more than one alcoholic beverage at night</li><li>Stop sleeping in</li></ul>

SHIFT	IMPLEMENTATION
SHIFT Drinking Soda **TO** Drinking one gallon water	No longer buy soda and purchase reusable water bottle
SHIFT Eating junk food **TO** Organic food	Going organic food shopping weekly
SHIFT Sleeping in **TO** Exercising for 30 minutes	Finding a trainer for a workout program

Stack It

We all love to hear the great big orchestral pieces played in movies that truly capture the moments. In music, the way this happens is by doing something we call stacking. After one take is deemed clean to the ear of the producer, the musicians are asked to replay the same exact section in order to accentuate what has already been played. The beauty of this is the fact that when the same frequencies link in sound, the size and depth of it grows exponentially. So, when an orchestra does two or three stacks, it sounds more like a hundred orchestras because of the expansion rate.

One part of evaluation that we cannot really comprehend or anticipate is this same exact method when it involves our habits and, eventually, our goals. The continuation of the healthy habits daily and the success rate of achieving our goals will almost be unfathomable because everything will begin to fall in place. This is where sayings like "they became rich overnight" or "the rich gets richer" comes from. There is a compound effect that takes place when you stack habits. Now this same effect works with the negative as well so it is imperative that you only reinforce the positive habits created. Once you have a routine that you deem clean, stack it for the days to come and be prepared for the overflow of success to come your way exponentially.

It is true that you can be your worst critic sometimes, but it is a very important part of exceeding your potential. If you always think that what you do is good enough then you will never aspire to be better. That is one of the reasons why those that are successful never get into the realm of significance. They start beginning to believe in their own advertisement. People around them praise them and tell them how great they are, leading to them believing it too strongly. This inevitably leads to their priorities changing from getting better to getting the praise. As the expectations remain the same, the effort put in decrease. There is no such thing as a plateau. We are either progressing or we are regressing. If you want to always be in the latter, here is what you must remember:

There is no such thing as a plateau. You are either fighting to make things better or you are fighting to stop them from getting worse.

Always remember your goals: *We have a tendency to forget what we are striving to become once we are in the midst of our* *daily routines. The habits we used to have still weigh heavily in our minds and makes it difficult to make the physical shift into something more. I mean we have all been there before. Buying that doughnut with your coffee and just before you bite into it, you remember you are on a diet. Going straight to bed once you get home and the next morning slapping yourself because you said you were going to read. It is human nature to forget things sometimes and that is okay. Living in the 21st century allows us to prevent that to the best of our possibilities though. So put down your goals everywhere. The first place I always tell people to put it is on their bathroom mirror. Let's be honest, we all look into that thing at least once a day. Grab a whiteboard marker and write your goals for the month and week on your bathroom mirror so you can look at your goals once a day as well. Set reminders on your phone. Change the background on your computer to something motivational. Tell your friends to slap you whenever you think about cheating. The opportunities are endless for us to remember them and it will not be long before you reach a point where you no longer have to be reminded. That is the point when the behavior becomes who you are.*

Your purpose is not just about presenting it well, but about making it better.

I will remind you that these goals are based on purpose. Although the rewards will be great for achieving them, the journey an the person you become throughout it supersedes the destination. The only way to make things better is by remembering what your goals were and knowing why you made them, regardless of what accolades the world gives you. It allows you to focus on your personal gain in purpose instead of your personal gain in success.

Always remember your thoughts: *What we think is what we get. We all know that our thoughts are the seeds planted for our actions. There will be moments that you will do something crazy,* *both good and bad. But, the only way to repeat (or not repeat) it again is by understanding why it came about in the first place. The origin of the motion is more important than the motion itself. Similar to the talents story spoken earlier in this book, the thought behind the things you do always wins. Have a journal and log your days. I personally like to have a virtual journal where I sit in front of my computer and video record me talking about my day so I can really see, hear, and feel how I was during the recording. Preventing a bad decision or having a good one reoccur is more likely when you understand why you did it in the first place. Remember to focus on the why.*

The origin of the motion is more important than the motion itself.

Always remember your legacy: *One of the reasons people tends to make character mistakes are because they forget who it is that they want to be. What happens in the present seems more important than the future. When you are judging yourself, it is important that you always judge as if you are that man/woman at the garden party.*

Making sure that everything you do sticks within the characteristics you claim to have is just as important as doing them.

Self-evaluation is vital in our growth and requires a lot of inward study and critique, which can lead to a lot of self-bashing. Although it is important to learn about your performance, it is equally as important to keep your self-esteem high in the process.

While watching a segment on television about Alabama Football during their reign as champions in the NCAA, there was a discussion, with Nick Saban, their head coach, about how he goes about making his team so phenomenal. Coach Saban explained how he encourages during losses and failures, and is really tough on his players when they are winning. His theory was that his team was at such a high level of performance that there was no need to beat up on the team when they lost because they already understood that they, well, lost. The constructive criticism during the time would always have a pick-me-up somewhere because the standard to excel was such a priority. In the program, anything that was done "wrong" did not need to stay a negative due to the lesson learned and words of encouragement.

On the other side of the coin, he believed (and I agree) that the greatest enemy of growth is success because the more fortune we collect, the less action we distribute. The stereotypical loud and obnoxious football coach that yells until he is red in the face would be the coach that would come out during their success because he wanted the team to exceed their potential. He wants the team he coaches and his time as their coach to be remembered and written down in the history books as one of the greatest dynasties in college football. He wanted to be significant.

Another thing we can do in evaluation is get a different point of view. Sometimes others catch what you miss better than you can. During the writing of this book, I gave my father a section that I wrote to see what he thought about it. I respect my father's opinion a lot and it was important for me to see what he thought about the material and the overall concept of the book. He is also a very honest person that never holds back any punches so as much as I wanted him to let me know how it was, I did not want him to at the same time. As he read, he suddenly paused for a moment and just looked at me.

With fear in my heart and a lump in my throat, I asked him what was wrong and he replied, "I think you need to find a way to copyright this stuff now before you send it to an editor."

Talk about pride and surprise all at the same time! When I heard that, I did not hear his praise, but his confirmation that what I was doing is in line with my purpose. The words he read and the thoughts that came into his mind went with the very things I was shooting for, and that lead me to write a lot faster. The truth may hurt sometimes, but the same pain can give you joy when seeing that it is there to help you. Good, bad, or indifferent, it is important to take what you can out of all of it by eating the meat, spitting out the bones, and finding ways to reach your goals.

Key Points

- Think positively when creating your goals, be specific, write them in first person, and in present tense.
- When creating the habits to accomplish your goals, make the **shift** from the poor habits to the good ones.
- Set your goals and stay on track because if you do **not** then the world will continue to pass you by and you will continuously get the results that you *do not* want.
- "Success is not to be pursued; it is to be attracted by the person you become" and that person grows each day when you take the time to nurture your future significant self.
- The odds of us getting what we want each day are higher when we are focused on getting it.
- The *only* thing in life that you cannot get more of is time.
- There is no such thing as a plateau. You are either fighting to make things better or you are fighting to stop them from getting worse.
- Your purpose is not just about presenting it well, it is about making it better.
- The origin of the motion is more important than the motion itself.

Performance: Significance

Dig Deeper

The success in our self-evaluation is what allows us to have the significance in our character as we become high performers. Write five goals in each category that you want to accomplish:

GOAL:	
Description of WHO I AM GOING TO BE	
New and current good habits to dig DEEP into	Poor habits I am going to stop
SHIFT	IMPLEMENTATION

Educational	Family	Influential	Experimental

Now it is time to form the physical behavior to meet these goals. Pick one goal from each category and fill out the Goal Digger Shift Form:

This is an uphill battle that requires a lot of self-evaluation with these specific thoughts in mind. Write down how you will implement each of the following thoughts.

Always remember your goals which are:
Always remember your thoughts which are:
Always remember your legacy which is:

Reverberation

If there is one thing that every musician should experience, it is time in the studio. You want to really talk about evaluation and getting higher by critiquing yourself, then there is no better judge than putting your talent on tape and listening to the playback thereafter. Time in the studio with the *Voices of Lee* was a monster that cannot be explained with such common things as words. We would go in as early as the sun would rise and leave as late as the stars would remain just to hopefully (keyword is hopefully) come out with *one* song.

We would go on and on for hours and hours, until every one of us wished that the power would go out, be a state of emergency, or anything to force us out of there.

"You do not want to come back to this twenty years from now and regret your efforts today," said our director when the hours began to weigh on our bodies.

That one moment would last for a lifetime as our voices from that one-day on echoes throughout eternity. That is why reverberation is such an important factor in a performer's life. Such an important factor in *your* life.

Reverberation is when something is reflected many times. It is a term mostly used in relation to echoes and the acoustics of an area and that is why it is the word I use to refer to making an impact. Reverberating is the continuation of a sound even when the source has stopped. The action resonates even when you are no longer around. One thing that we must realize as high performers is that we cannot achieve our goals and exceed by ourselves. From Bill Gates and Paul Allen to Jesus and the twelve disciples, those that remain throughout history, even after they walk away from their purpose, have it reverberating throughout the ages because others make it happen. In conjunction to that, these people always have others impact their lives and are capable of doing the same for those they can reach. There are four aspects of reverberation that high performers are constantly making a part of who they are:

1. Mentors
2. Teams
3. Networks
4. Charity

Having constant interaction in each of these links is what creates the capacity necessary to exceed your potential. We all have dreams and goals that are bigger than us as it should be and we can assure that it reverberates in the mind of others to join us. Let's start making the echo that will outlive us.

Mentors

We are all here to raise the bar every time we possibly can. No matter what we accomplish, there is a natural auger as a living thing that pushes us to do more and be more. Plants grow as much as they can, cows produce as much milk as they can, even the Earth itself supplies enough oxygen as it can. But, in order for us to excel in life, we need mentors to help push us when we reach a plateau or a sticking point.

The word mentor is defined as a trusted counselor, teacher or influential supporter. There aren't too many people in our world that can say that they got to where they are without a coach or a supportive parent and here is the reason why we need those type of people in our lives.

A mentor is a cheat sheet to your place of significance

First, a mentor can give us experience. When we begin to live out our purpose, an experience mentor in your field of practice is capable of helping us. A mentor is there to give us the pointers necessary when we run into new territory because they have already been there. In essence, they help us avoid the pitfalls and learning in the school of hard knocks by giving us a map of the area that helps us see the shortcuts.

Second, a mentor can give us an ear. During the initial struggles, there will be a lot of people that are currently around you that cannot even fathom what you are trying to attempt. They are so focused on the funny video on their newsfeed and what they are going to wear at the club that when you talk to them about what you have to go through, they will only give you negative feedback. A mentor can sit down with you and listen to your woes because they have been there. The empathy they portray is genuine and will help you get back up when you are knocked down.

Third, a mentor gives us accountability. A mentor is a realistic version of Big Brother. The goals you lay out before you become their goals because they want you to succeed almost as much as you do. If you are slacking off, they will be sure to bring the rod and beat you back into shape. If you meet your goals, they will ask you what the next step is for you in your progression. A mentor is there to help you continually rise and prevent any fall. There are three kinds of mentors and obtaining all of them would be beneficial in every way.

1. Everyday Mentor
2. Hands-On Mentor
3. Hero Mentor

The Everyday Mentor

Life comes at us in all types of ways every single day. Most people do not take much notice to an interaction with someone in the grocery line or the commercial that comes on, but every and any thing that we run into is a possible teacher. People and experiences, when we are open and have the passion to learn, can allow us to discover marvelous things that will assist us in our pursuit of high performance. We have all seen a movie or show with a protagonist running out of ideas and "accidentally" discovering one because of what someone says or something they see. This "accident" is not one at all. There persistence and tenacity for the discovery is what gives them the opportunity to discover. The analogies and references in this book alone are a great example of that. From life stories to comic books, the world I personally live in is full of learning opportunities *because* I am continuously searching for those opportunities. The Everyday Mentor is often overlooked, but it is the most accessible and the one that can really help you achieve your goals not only because of the lessons learned, but also because it reminds you that the answers you seek truly are inside you. You just need a little jarring every once in a while.

The Hands-On Mentor

The second kind of mentor is the Hands-On Mentor. Remember the society and superior groups in the doubt section? Well this type of mentor comes from those groups. Whether it is your college professor, your best friend or a parent, a hands-on mentor is someone that you have one-on-one encounters with often and intentionally. These mentors, in the early stages of our lives, tend to just appear, like your choir director or that uncle that is super successful. As we get older and, more specifically, walk away from traditional education, it is much more difficult to find these type of mentors. These mentors are often people we work for, with and even pay. In spite of how you find one of these coaches, it is imperative that you do your best to get them to prioritize your goals because they too are usually pushing to exceed their potential. Do what you can to support their needs and be a part of their focus in order for you to be a part of theirs. It is in giving that we receive.

The Hero Mentor

The last (and my personal favorite) kind of mentor is the Hero Mentor. These giant figures that are as grand as the gods seated on Mount Olympus. Their success in what they do in their respective fields and who they are as people is what you strive to become. They are Big Brother's bigger brothers (and sisters of course). A lot of these mentors may not be accessible because they are so big or perhaps they are historical figures or fictional characters. Regardless of who they are and where they come from, the idea is that these guys are similar to the Dream Team. You know, the 1992 US Olympic Basketball Team that featured active NBA players

Performance: Significance

for the first time. The Dream Team that starred Michael Jordan, Larry Bird and Magic Johnson (just to name a few). Similar to that Dream Team, your team should have all those that you consider to be the greats.

Come up with at least twelve figures, either past, present, or fictional, that you would want to be like. After you come up with this group of names, research them all. Read articles and biographies. Watch documentaries and put their pictures on your wall the same way you had boy band and celebrity crushes on your wall. Then, when you hit a rough patch or coming up in new territory, think to yourself what they would do. Ask questions and think what their responses would be. Your Dream Team is their to council you as you go leaps and bounds over what anyone could ever imagine. Over anything *you* could have imagined.

Teams

Another way high performers create reverberation is by forming a team. Most of us, if not all of us will need to create a team at some point in time as we exceed our potential because our purpose will get too big for one person to handle. If you look at the life of any successful person, they all reached their significant life with a team of some sort. Bill Gates and Paul Allen started Microsoft. Tom Brady and Bill Belichik won four Super Bowls. The Jackson 5. Even Jesus had the twelve disciples! Significant people always create a team that is capable of achieving their goals faster and more sufficiently which leads to designing even bigger ones to accomplish. Due to the fact that these individuals you find have the same morals and values as you, you are all capable of working together because you are all wanting the same outcomes. The combined energy of the whole is what pushes your talents, opportunities, goals, and abilities to greater heights.

Now a "team" is capable of great things, but let's dig a little deeper to a more family-based group. From rappers to athletes, the word "team" has a much more in depth meaning and value when it is what those born in the 21st century call a "squad." A squad is a dedicated and committed group that supports you and your goals in a positive manner. These people are the ride or die type that not only support you, but you support them as well as everyone strives to raise the bar both as a group and as individuals. These brothers and sisters in arms are the extra push needed to let your purpose reverberate throughout the world.

Creating Your Squad

Throughout our entire lives, we have been taught to work on our weaknesses. If you were not good at math, you would go to a tutor. If your public speaking is not as great as you want it to be, you go to an instructor or research speakers online. What is necessary for a squad is the complete opposite. The purpose of finding these goal diggers around you is so they can work on all the things you are not that great at. The idea is for each person to focus on their strengths and work on the tasks that they are best at. StrengthsFinder states that there are four domains of leadership strength. All of these strengths are necessary to be a part of your squad in order for the reverb to take full effect.

Discovering your strength(s) is the first step to discover a team to support you.

1. **Executor**
2. **Influencer**
3. **Relationship Builder**
4. **Strategic Thinker**

As an illustrator to describe exactly what each strength is designed to do on your squad, I am going to use the original squad of high productivity…in the fictitious world.

The Justice League

1. Strategic Thinker (Batman): A strategic thinker is capable of analyzing a scenario, discovering and creating the most effective plan of action. One of the most well-known figures of this is Batman. This superhero is the only person in the original Justice League that does not have any super powers. What makes him a forced to be reckoned with is his intelligence. Being one of the only people to defeat Superman and having known knowledge to defeat just about anybody, Batman is capable of taking any plan and/or idea and forming a strategy that will allow the squad to succeed. The Batman in your squad might often be considered a cynic and one that does not have much faith in anything, but how they break every idea and thought down is what makes them capable of building them back up to be better than before.
2. Influencer (Wonder Woman): What many people do not realize is that Wonder Woman's uniform was intentionally designed as a way to influence others. Wonder Woman, as the ambassador warrior from a different world, wears the American colors to represent her and her birthplace's allegiance to the United States and their ideals of freedom and democracy. An influencer is there to have others believe in the team's cause and want to be a part in any way possible. From investors to additions to the every day work the squad has to complete, an influencer markets your purpose in an effective way.
3. Executor (Superman): Superman is borderline the most powerful being in the world of fiction. His abilities are endless (flight, x-ray vision, heat vision, enhanced hearing, etc.) and the strength of these powers are limitless (because there is a time the man was capable of moving an entire planet). The person that is deemed Superman on your team will definitely be honored to be considered the

executor. An executor is the one capable of converting the plan into action. In essence, the executor is the physical behavior to the strategic thinker's mental behavior. No matter what the circumstances are, these people will find a way to get things done and are a very crucial part of your squad. As the urban culture says, this person knows how to "do work, son."

4. Relationship Builder (Flash): As ironic as it may be, the relationship builder is the last on this list and the one that embodies him best in the Justice League is the Flash. The Flash is usually depicted as one of the youngest members of this team and is friends with everyone on it, almost always being one of the first to learn the secret identity of the fellow members. The reason why is because a relationship builder is the glue that connects everyone else. These different strengths include different personalities and there is a need for some one to be cohesive and remind everyone that we are all doing this together as a squad. Not only is a relationship builder great for internal affairs, but they are great for external ones as well. These people are also great with customer services and assuring that everyone that your squad comes in contact with feels comfortable and wanting your business the next time around.

We all have one or more of these strengths and are capable of executing tasks that are best suited to them. After discovering your strength and your squad's strengths, high productivity relies in the proper division of tasks. Once you (or whoever is your strategic thinker) does this, you have officially created another level of reverberation.

Networks

The next way to have your purpose multiply is by using the most simple form of all four of our methods and that is by networking. The reason why networking is so simple is because this era makes it so, not to mention that it is continuously growing when used properly.

1. Your Network

We *all* have some form of network. Family, friends, co-workers, ex-girlfriend(s), we are all connected to a lot of people and, thanks to social media, it is even easier to stay connected. The concept of networking has different mathematical terminology from Metcalfe's Law all the way to the infamous Six Degrees of Separation. Regardless of how you depict it, the concept is simple in terms of being high performers: *Who we know can geometrically effect our success.*

2. Their Network

The next networking group is the contacts your network have. If those in your life told just five people about who you are and what you are doing to make a difference in the world, your reverb will be you yelling at the Grand Canyon big. People that you do not know, but have mutual friends with you could discover you simply because what you do came up in conversation. What is most important about this network is letting *Your Network* to know what you do, have information on how to find you, and find a way to connect. One of the biggest things you learn in sales is that there are a lot of people, companies, and organizations that sell your product or services. The reason why people may not necessary buy what you do is because they cannot buy who you are first. In essence, they do not trust you because they do not *know* you. But, if your mother knows you sell houses and then she talks to her girlfriend on the phone that is looking for a new home, you have officially tapped into *Their Network*. It amazes me how many of us have friends that we hang out with or family members we see at times and we do not really know what they do. There is an entire pool of people within your camp that you do not even know about yet and it is simply because you have yet to allow others be a part of your purpose. Let them in and allow someone else to be a blessing to you.

3. Discovered Network

This group of people are the ones you find throughout life. We run into people every single day and always have random conversations. Whether it is with the guy sitting next to you on the plane or the lady taking your order, we run into a plethora of individuals daily. But, since most people do not like public speaking and definitely do not like speaking to strangers, we miss out on the opportunity. Now giving someone your elevator pitch right out the gate is not the idea. This is more about making a *connection*. The Discovered Network comes from meeting new people and then keeping in contact with them. The focus is always about how you can help them first as oppose to how they can help you. Find what you have in common with them and become acquainted. What is most important is forming the relationship so they shift from being in the Discovered Network to the Your Network category. Not to mention having a few more good people in your life never hurts either.

4. Infinte Network

My favorite of all the networks is this one right here. The Infinite Network are the people that are looking for *you*. Yes, that is right, there are people in this world that are looking for exactly what you do. *Your purpose was created to better the world, right?* There are people all over wanting you to help them with their needs. Our job is to make sure they can find us. Create a website (because it is easy and free these days). Have information about yourself on social media. Even dropping off business cards and flyers in the local stores in your area could do wonders that you cannot even imagine! Your Infinite Network is the universe following the law that with every action, there is an equal and opposite one. The hardworking hours and continuous push to exceed your potential comes back around here. This is the seed that you cannot see because it is buried in the ground. As long as you have faith in who you are (your preparation) and do what you can to be there at the opportune moment, the Infinite Network will always be there to support you.

Charity

The last and final form of reverberation is by far the most important. If you ask any successful person name three things that make them so significant in this world, charity would be one of them. Having the capacity to give to others is an art that is not discussed often enough in our society. When living a purpose-driven life, charity is what allows others to have the opportunity to live a purpose-driven life as well. In Scripture, we are told to give 10% of our earnings back in order to support those less fortunate and this is something that I believe. What I believe those that exceed their potential do is give 10% back in their craft as well. Now this will look different for each person, but the idea is to do what you do without cost. So take the contracting job at the community center and surprise them with a 10% discount or go to the local university and give a free lecture. Find a child that you can mentor or go visit a nursing home and play games with the tenants once a month. Giving 10% of your finances can be easy and just be another number in the books because the people you are really giving to do not see it. Giving 10% of your time to help them or even just visit will be a memory they won't ever forget.

One of my favorite moments ever was going to Jamaica on a Missions Trip. My father and I lived on the ridges of the Blue Mountains in a village, giving medical treatment from dusk till dawn every single day for an entire week. We helped the kids bring back clean water from the stream. We took trips to Kingston to tell people that they have a purpose in life and they should do their best to discover it. We even helped our hosts with their chores around the village. It would have been easy to just give some money for the trip expenses and there is nothing wrong with that. But visiting those you support financially, even just one time, will change your life forever.

You are the average of the five people you spend the most time with

Reverberation is really about relationships. Not too long ago, I was on a road trip to Tennessee to help move my sister's things out of my house. When we stopped at a gas station, we went inside to pick up a few things for the final leg of our trip. Now I do not remember what we talked about when we reached the cash register, but that lady had us going for a few minutes longer than we had anticipated. We all laughed and had a good time, but it didn't seem to be anything serious, to us at least. Days later, we had to stop at that same gas station for fuel. When I walked in, the lady at the cash register was so delighted to see me. We actually talked even longer the second time around and she thanked me for being so kind. Here again, I did not think anything of it, but the little things in life really do make the biggest difference. There are people that I do not see for years that come up to me with a smile on their face because of how I made them feel. They do not always remember what I did, but they always remember who I am and how I treated them. High performers understand that every part of the show is important. The guy pulling the curtain is just as important to them as the audience paying for the tickets because it all coincides within their purpose. Back to loving others as yourself, you treat people not the way they are supposed to be treated, but the way *you* would want to be treated. A person with great character and significance understands that we are all God's children so it is important to appreciate others in that light.

Jim Rohn stated that "you are the average of the five people you spend the most time with" and there is not a doubt in my mind that he is right. The one thing I have yet to mention is that reverberation goes both ways. As much as you are echoing out, there is still a vibration coming back to your being as well. It is important that the source is continuously feeding itself positivity and the only way to do that is to have good company around you. It is imperative that the source of the reverb constantly sends out a positive tone. The people you meet are there to receive it and the people you surround yourself are there to feed you, the source, in order for you to continue the process.

Key Points:

- Reverberation is the continuation of your purpose by growing a community to support you.
- Mentors are there to help guide you as you become a high level performer.
- Your team is there to be strong where you are weak. Find a squad that will be a part of your purpose.
- Networks are there to help tell your story. Find new ways to state your purpose and do your best to let others know what you do.
- It is in giving that we receive so find ways to be charitable in the lives of others.

Dig Deeper:

- Making sure everything you do sticks within the characteristics you claim to have is just as important as doing them.
- Maya Angelou said, "People will forget what you said, people will forget what you did, but people will never forget how you made them feel."

- Make a list of five people that you would like to have as a Hands-On Mentor and make a plan to have at least one as a mentor. Use the Goal Digger Shift Form to assist you.
- Who is your Dream Team? Make a list of twelve Hero Mentors that you look up to. After doing this, find some form of literature (autobiography, documentary, article, etc.) about them and read one for each month. Have their pictures and/or quotes hanging up around your office as a way to remind you that they are there to help you as you reverberate your purpose.
- Who is your Squad? Make a list of people that you want to be a part of your squad that works alongside you. Work together to discover each other's strengths and align the tasks respectively.
- Make a list of ten friends in your network that could help spread the word about your trade. After that, ask then to contact five more people to tell about the news.
- Work on your Discovered Network by finding a business meet-and-greet in your area. Make it a goal to visit it at least once a month.
- Learn new ways to help your Infinite Network find out what you do and who you are.

Pick three charities you would like to support and how you will support them. Remember that giving time is just as meaningful as giving finances.

Chapter 16

Following Up and Opening Up

High performance phenoms seem to never fail to reach their accomplishments. We are capable of making calculated decisions that allow us to successfully connect our purpose with the purpose of others. By understanding where they are in their life and going to them to give a helping hand throughout the process is a basis that we create by following up.

When I made the decision to leave the *Voices of Lee* and make my own path in life, I was distraught. The night before a studio recording session, I tossed and turned all night as my head began to fill with questions and concerns about my future. When dawn broke, there was no grand enlightenment that came along with it. Needless to say, I went to the studio still confused and lost. One of my best buds, (who is really good at following up), somehow noticed my pain, although no one else seemed to recognize it because (I have a habit of hiding my emotions and moments of perplexity). After asking me what was wrong and me not really explaining the situation, he did not do anything more than simply say that he was there for me, which is what we are discussing.

Following up is split into three separate ideas:

Following To
Following Through
Following Up

These very important aspects of selflessness connects us to others and grows our spiritual behavior because it is a representation of relating and associating ourselves with people we interact with.

Following To

An art that has been lost in these recent years is empathy. Empathy is synonymous with understanding and relating. One of the reasons for this is because people like to group empathy with sympathy and although they are similar, they are quite different as well. Sympathy is a form of agreement and to agree with someone or thing, you have to reflect your thoughts and emotions which is not empathy. Empathy is an understanding that does not relate you, but relates to what they are going through. What we are trying to do is embody the other person/thing and put ourselves in their shoes essentially. We are looking at it from their perspective, not ours. Most of us, when we are in a conversation, are not listening to understand, but listening to respond. As the other party picks and chooses their words, we are doing the exact same thing regarding our response, which is not "following to." In order to "follow to," you cannot listen with just your ears.

Two of my favorite television series are *Psych* and *Lie to Me*. The first television show is about a crime consultant with observational skills that I would die for (figuratively of course). This comedic drama's lead role takes this talent, along with his detective skills, to solve these cases as a "psychic" because he is attentive to his surroundings. In the other show, *Lie to Me*, Dr. Cal Lightman is an applied psychology expert that focuses on micro-expressions, body language, voice pitch, and so on as a crime consultant and a deception expert. These two characters take empathy to the next level by listening with all of their senses (sight, touch, taste, smell, and hearing) in congruence with their desire to get into the heads of others.

The days of telling people, "I know exactly how you feel" and "I did the very same thing one time," are over. What we must do to follow to is discover the stuff behind the stuff, and we can only do that by clarifying everything in any given situation. We must understand that our spiritual behavior is designed to communicate with the heart and mind of another. It is in connecting to *who* they are that we can understand and meet them where they are in order to have a place of significance in their life.

"Following to" is a sacrifice because you are only focusing on the person and situation at hand.

By understanding where they are, you can then properly help them out with their needs because it is then, when you follow to their thoughts and feelings, even when you don't not see eye-to-eye, you can see through their eyes and understand the purpose of any action in any situation.

Following Through

A person of character will always keep intact one thing throughout their lives and that is their word. A person of character knows that their word is their bond and will keep that truth consistent. Following through is the belief that everyone's time and energy is just as valuable as your own so you treat it as such. My father, (God bless his soul), has a lot of great characteristics and lives a life of significance, but one thing that he has always struggled with is being on time. In spite of the stereotypes that portray black folk, especially Caribbean folk, as late, he is the only one in my family that practices such notions (I promise you).

One day, when I was getting on to him for being late for a meeting, he responded, "What's the big deal? It's not like they are going to start without us.".

My father is also a very intelligent man, but we all have our moments. "The issue is not them beginning without us, Dad," I pointed out, "the issue is how selfish we will be by showing up later than when we had said because now their time table will be off because we are; not to mention that our tardiness shows lack of preparation because it is impossible to hop out of the car after thinking about how late you are and automatically think about the conversation you will have in the meeting. But, more importantly, if we said we are going to show up at a certain time, then we need to show up at that time in spite of how others respond to it." (Yes I sometimes call my father out. I'm bigger than him so he can't really put the switch on me.)

It is imperative that we are reliable because that is what high performers are. Many of us are pretty good with following through in terms of engagements and promises, but if we dig a little deeper, we will see that it is also important that we follow through with our beliefs and values as well.

One moment in my life that always challenges my character is driving. Road rage is a very mild way of describing my tendencies. Be it that my foot has lead in it as soon as I am behind the wheel, you can use your imagination to know where I am coming from. Oh, and it does not help that I come from the Tri-State area (New York, New Jersey, Pennsylvania) either. My initial instincts when driving used to be cut people off, cuss people out, and have the notion that the speed limit and traffic signs were more suggestions for the jokers that cannot drive.

But, when I started to focus more on living a life of significance, that all had to change. Texting became a thing of the past because 1) I didn't not want to put lives in danger, and 2) I can'not really try and be in tune with someone on the follow to habit of our spiritual behavior if I am also attempting to do so on the road to avoid a catastrophic wreck while driving. Although my speeding still resides, it has gotten better and I now like to make up stories for people whenever they are not driving up to my standard. If someone cuts me off then they might be running late for work or about to have a birth inside their vehicle so they are rushing to the hospital. A slow driver is probably an older individual just living the high life or have some precious cargo in the car. Regardless, I have started to use the "follow to" process to work on my "follow through."

Following Up

Imagine you are going on a date with a lovely gentleman (or woman, depending on the way you role). You go out and have a great dinner which had a great conversation and lead to you two having a great time. Everything you would ever want to experience on a date, happened and your date was all you have ever hoped for. As they respectfully take you home and wish you a goodnight, they drove off into the distance as you recollect how amazing the evening was. The average person would expect a phone call the next day after hitting things off so well the night before, right? Well, what if they did not call? Actually, you never hear from them again. How confusing would that be?! After such a wonderful time, you would expect them to follow up and possibly attempt to recreate the experience.

If you are agreeing with me on this date, then why don't we do this with the all the "dates" in our lives?

Following up is going the extra mile and keeping the spiritual bond that we have established with another person.

How often do we have a wonderful meeting with a client or conversation with a friend and forget to restate our appreciation? I know it may seem like a small thing, but the little things are what count. Think about all of the times someone did something you were not expecting and how that impacted your life. A bouquet of flowers or a random phone call from a friend will be the one thing you will remember for weeks, even if it was "just a small gesture.".

During my initiation in the world of speaking and writing, my first coach was a man named Jonathan Sprinkles. A great speaker and even better person, this man was the king of following up. Whenever he would run into something that reminded him of someone during his travels, he would get it for them or, at the very least, take a picture of it and let them know that he was thinking about them. He would send me hand-written postcards, random messages of encouragement, and even gave me a tie and a pair of his signature funky socks (as in style, not smell) that I actually wore during my very first talk. Every time this man would go to an engagement, he would always show his appreciation to the planner that booked him after. By having a giving spiritual behavior, you can be capable of doing all of these aspects of following up as you properly define your character by acting it out.

It is in our concentration to be a blessing to someone that another will be a blessing to us in return. It is in sowing these seeds that we can eventually reap their benefits.

Opening Up

An aspect of life that most of us avoid is openness. Our lives being presented on the big screen for all to witness is definitely not on the to-do list, no matter how often we may say we want to be "famous." Lights and glamour are the desires of the attention-hungry folk that want people in their face when they want them to, but it never works that way. Following to, following through, and following up involved us understanding others first before they understood us and meeting them where they are.

Opening to, opening through, and opening up is how we allow our lives to be used as an example to impact the lives of others, including our own.

People who want fame never want others to know who they really are because there is no substance behind their closed doors, both figuratively and literally. People who want significance let their lifestyle be known to our society even with past mistakes because we understand that our less than prideful endeavors, prior to our shift into digging deep, has the capacity to guide another person out or away of a similar circumstance.

Opening To

Opening to is saying yes to new ideas and opportunities when we have no idea what may come out of them.

These moments can be as simple as a friend calling you up for a bite to eat or as grand as becoming the CEO of a Fortune 500 company. It is derived from the phrases, "I am opening up to the idea of," or "I am open to the opportunity of". The factor that separates us from these moments takes us back to our mental behavior and our separation from doubts and excuses. If we have the time and energy to tackle these occasions, we should do our best to avoid uncertainty and our comfort to take a chance. The question has been raised for a reason and every question is an opportunity.

My new discovery in life has come through a series of questions and me opening up to each opportunity. After taking my leap of faith by leaving my singing group and walking away from what I call home, Tennessee, I did not have the slightest clue in knowing what to do next. I knew that what had been done, needed to be done, but I was as blind as a bat in the brightness of my future. Each step taken was not one I had seen before and/or foreseen. After getting a job (for bills sake) and moving to New Jersey, I continued to search for the next opportunity and found nothing. It was not until I met family that I never knew existed that the ball started to roll.

Three months after my life-changing decision into the next chapter in my purpose, a few cousins of mine from California ended up at my doorstep on Independence Day. (Ironic, I know, but I promise you this is the truth. No one can make something like this up.) When we got to know each other, they gave me the opportunity to visit them in San Diego for a personal development conference, and boy did I develop. Those three days were the very thing I had been searching for the last three months and was used to begin the domino effect as follows:

I left San Diego and was given another opportunity, but this time to go to Dallas with the great T.D. Jakes in MegaFest. It was there that I met Jonathan Sprinkles, the coach I spoke to you earlier about, who also had an event, but this one for speakers, out in Houston. I went to MegaFest with my father and he wanted to know if I wanted to go to Jonathan's Presentation Power event in Houston, which I excitedly obliged to because I continuously wanted to be open to and step in faith. It was a few months later in Houston that I was given the opportunity to join Mr. Sprinkles and have him be my coach. That is how I discovered a few small gems in my story that can be used to be a person of significance.

It was also there that I received another opportunity to return to Houston and be a part of a focus group, which I also agreed to be associated with. *That* is where I decided to go out on a limb and write this book you have in your hand, lap, table, or whichever way you are holding it. All of these layers, in a span of about six months, are what got me to write the first words to those that want to dig deep and live a high performance life of significance because I too wanted to live such a life. If I ever questioned who I was and/or decided to choose my comfort over the obvious place in priority these moments had in my purpose and potential, who knows where I would be today, let alone this book.

Opening Through

As noted, i equates to our strong mental behavior and how we use it to say "yes" to opportunities. *Opening through* is actually showing up wholeheartedly by properly implementing our physical behavior(s). If there is one thing that I love and hate at the same time, it would be the wondrous cell phone. These things, that were made to make our lives easier, are now just distractions as we use them *all the time* for what is usually recreation. More importantly, we use them at the worst times ever for the worst reasons ever.

From texting in the middle of a movie to talking on the phone when you're ordering food (which servers loathe), our mobile devices and other gadgets have made us lose the moment. Opening through is about being somewhere wholeheartedly.

It is one thing to actually show up to an engagement. It is another thing to actually be *engaged* in the engagement you are in.

I mean, come on people. Is it not annoying to you to be doing/ or saying something and the person you are with is paying little to no attention to you?

Is it not frustrating to plan a great night with a group of friends to catch up and the only thing they want to catch up on is social media?

Am I the only one that believes it is a pain in the assets to drive past an individual with their hand connected to their head like a Siamese as they are going ten miles an hour under the speed limit?

Here again, if you would not want it to happen to you then why do you do it to others?

More importantly, how much do we miss when we do not open through?

Even more importantly, how much of our character do we miss when we do not open through?

People with strong character take advantage of moments that they can use to set an example and be a representative of positive actions.

People that understand and respect purpose know that each occasion has its own purpose and is vital in their development.

A person that has the zeal to exceed their potential recognizes that they can get one step closer by taking in everything that surrounds them.

We must remember that communication has very little to do with what is said. The only way to use our others senses is by ingoring the distractions and being engaged in the now. That is the way significant folk (like you and me) roll.

Opening Up

We know that it is important to understand another's heart, mind, and soul in order to have their insight within their circumstances. When it comes time for us to be understood and take what we have learned to help them, how do we go about it? The solution for kindred spirits comes in our spiritual behavior by us opening up the windows to our own heart, mind, and soul. When we give every bit of knowledge and wisdom we have for any situation, we can assure that our role will be significant. This goes for all of our relationships, too. Whether personal or business, when we let people into our world and give them our insight, we give them a chance of success, especially when the situation took us to the school of hard knocks.

From an organizational standpoint, these are the products and services you have to offer. As a parent, this is letting your kids know that you actually screwed up to and can relate. With your new boyfriend, this is admitting to your past *in the beginning* to allow them to understand who you really are. Each title or "how" has its own place for opening up and each position requires an environment of high risk, but our foundation of character gives us a peace of mind for such things. The culmination of all these things creates an atmosphere that allows us to truly help people.

When we try and give snippets of what our life has to offer then the world will give us snippets in return because every action gives us an equal reaction.

It is natural for us to actively give just a little because we want to protect ourselves. However, it is hard to do so when your arms are up in the air signaling your openness. The highly trained Marines of America are dangerous as long as they are still breathing because their character can uphold even the worst situations. They are so good at what they do that, as people, they are considered weapons in a court of law. They are good enough to put themselves out in

Following Up and Opening Up

the open and still survive, if not thrive when they face adversity. We must be the same in our purpose and all three of our behaviors in order to be high performers and significant people.

Key Points

- "Following to" is a sacrifice because you only focus on the person and situation at hand.
- Following up is going the extra mile and keeping the spiritual bond that we have established with another party relative.
- It is in our concentration to be a blessing to someone that another will be a blessing to us in return. It is in sowing these seeds that we can eventually reap their benefits.
- Opening to is us saying yes to new ideas and opportunities when we have no idea what may come out of them.
- It is one thing to actually show up to an engagement. It is another thing to actually be *engaged* in the engagement you are in.
- When we try and give snippets of what our life has to offer then the world will give us snippets in return because every action gives us an equal reaction.

Dig Deeper

Would I want that to happen to me?
Am I representing my character?

Many of us are pretty good with following through in terms of engagements and promises, but if we dig a little deeper, we will see that we often fail to follow through with our beliefs and Big Brother characteristics.

Explain how this has been true in your life.

What are you going to change in this area as a result of reading this chapter?

Opening to, opening through, and opening up are how we allow our lives to be used as an opportunity to impact the lives of others. Explain how each one of these "openings" is going to operate in your own life from now on.

People with _____ _____ take advantage of moments that they can use to set an example and be a representative of positive actions.

People that _____ and _____ purpose know that each occasion has its own purpose and is vital in their development.

A person that has the zeal to _____ their _____ recognizes that they can get one step closer in doing so by taking in _____ that surrounds them.

Conclusion

Resting and Maintaining

I know, I know. People that are constantly thriving to accomplish more within their lives want to do anything *but* rest."

I mean, seriously? Taking time to get a little R&R in the midst of the controlled chaos called our lives that is laughable. Most of us are trying to squeeze even more work in so how is it possible to find moments of rest?

A time to rest is a time to rejuvenate your mind, body and spirit. Constantly moving without any time to take a moment for yourself will burn you out quickly. There are two forms of rest that are necessary for us because it is during those times that we can refocus and continue our process of exceeding potential.

Sabbath

The first form of resting takes root from when God created the heavens and the Earth. The Sabbath is a time mostly observed in Abrahamic religions where those of the faith take a day out of the week to rest. The most that they may do is take time to worship, but that is about as far as they are supposed to go. Such a rest day is designed for the people to acknowledge the works of the week that has passed and anticipate the works for the week to come. It is the one time out of the week where we are meant to enjoy life and prepare for what will come next. There are some extremes (for lack of a better word and not in terms of disrespect) to the Sabbath where some won't even flip on a light switch as the more liberal methods are designed to step away from an occupation or trade. Regardless of where you want to be, the Sabbath is practiced by work ending at nightfall and resuming the following evening at sundown. Throughout those twenty-four hours of rest, the only thing that any of us should really be paying attention to is family,, faith, and you. It is not a time to take care of errands or catch up on your tasks. It is designed for you to be grateful for what you have, reflect on has happened, and prepare for what is to come.

A friend a mine from the Dallas/Fort Worth area runs his own company, so the idea of a Sabbath was about as much of a fairytale in his life as the one that gives you a dollar for a lost tooth. The man would work constantly just to keep his business afloat and never had time to himself. A couple years back, he decided to go ahead and actually set one day a week to be deemed as his Sabbath. In the beginning, his efforts seemed to be counterproductive as he lost a few business opportunities, but boy did that change. After doing this for a few months, his company about doubled in revenue and he received more long-term business relationships than he ever had before. He told me how clearing his schedule for a day also cleared his mind and allowed him to be more alert when the time came. It is important for us to always take great strides to exceed our potential, but we cannot do that successfully if we are continuously driving on an empty tank. Even machines need to plug in and recharge.

Sabbatical

The cool, elongated version of the Sabbath is often known as a vacation or a getaway. Taking a few days, or even weeks, to either have a vacation or staycation (which is when you act like you are going away, but you just book a hotel in town). This is great because not only do you have time to yourself, you also get time away from your regular routine and environment. Changing scenery, even slightly, can change your perspective and allow you to really get a different outlook. Artistic individuals, especially ones that write novels and scripts, tend to leave their humble abodes when they are beginning to scribe the next great American masterpiece because a change in atmosphere naturally gives them a change in mind.

Celebrating

This is a bonus that I really want to talk about because it is another thing that highly productive people tend to dismiss from their mind. Celebrating is not a bad thing to do. Gathering colleagues and loved ones to rejoice after accomplishing something big in your life is important. It is especially great when you meet your goals and prepare to take the next step in exceeding them. It is a great moment to not only congratulate yourself, but also those that have supported you throughout the journey. Besides, we all enjoy a good party every once in a while.

Resting is an investment in yourself so you can have the strength to invest in others. Remember that all of this is meant for the bettering of our world. We cannot do that if we can barely get out of the bed and render our best. It is also necessary because it is a great way to celebrate the amount of successful effort you have put in. Our behaviors sometimes need to take some time to just sit back and relax. I mean come on people; even God took a chill pill after laying down the elbow grease.

Maintaining

Here's the thing. We have spoken about *a lot* of things and there is much to be done and done it shall be, but how do we maintain it? How often do we jump out the gates with a full head of steam and slowly, but surely, begin to frizzle out to nothing? We all have been a victim of making a New Year's Resolution that falls through the cracks before we even hit Valentine's Day or starting a program way better than we finished it. Human nature is constantly trying to keep things the way they always have been and avoid any scrutiny that could possibly lead to anything even remotely relevant to the word, change. Sorry to be blunt, but we are already running up the down escalator strictly due to the weak substance that we call our flesh. It's unfortunate, but who cares. We aren't looking for an easy life. We are obtaining a purposeful one. Maintaining our purpose-driven life is dependent more on the matter in between our ears and how we use it to create new paradigms for our life. Here are a few things we need to keep in mind in order to be consistent in character, purpose, performance at the highest level, behaviors, and, of course, exceeding our potential.

We Are Always Learners:

It is apparent that this concept is one that you know because if you didn't then you would not have picked up this book (or any book for that matter). A lot of us stop our education once we walk away with that really expensive piece of paper we spent however many years to receive while wearing that cap and gown that spikes your body temperature to sizzlin'. What we fail to recognize is that schooling is only supposed to be the foundation used to continuously build our knowledge and intelligence. We all have to remove that mentality sooner or later in order to truly reach, and exceed, our potential.

For me, I thought that high school and college was what separated me from starting my career and life as an adult. Those humanity courses and random classes like bowling necessary for me to have the right credits, both in terms of amount and in content, made me so frustrated when I was studying in school. I definitely did not get as much as I could have because my paradigm needed to be shifted. I always enjoyed learning, but I did not enjoy some "big shot" standing in the front of a room practically reading the textbook to me so I can practice my procrastination and cramming abilities when it was time to regurgitate the information. Sigh, ignorance is bliss. The truth of the matter is that those "random courses" were there to broaden the spectrum to see what else could be of interest and use to me.

Professors were there to support me and keep me on track with the material. Any form of test was not there to regurgitate the information just to be lost the next day, but a way to survey my study and work habits so I could adapt accordingly to better the potential in my work ethic and time management. (I bet a lot of us wish this was told to us back when we were in school.) These are the things we should be focusing on as we continue to learn after our school days are over. Now we have many more options and a lot more opportunities because we now have total control of our education. It is in our constant search for wisdom and knowledge that we can exceed our potential in order to have the positive response of significance and wealth in our lives.

Know That There is NO Plateau

When I was singing with the *Voices of Lee*, the one thing that I would always hear is how there is no such thing as a plateau. As human beings, we physically cannot be consistent *unless* we push to be so. If you bust your chops in the gym and pay attention to the way you eat this year and then just sit back and stop your training and nutrition regimen the following year, all of that hard work will go kaput as your gains (or losses) begin to decline back to the very bottom of the hill. Maintaining what you have achieved is not as much work, but still a good amount of effort is required because nothing just stays consistent in this world. Maintaining what we have achieved is not attractive to us. Instead, *maintaining to achieve* is a sexier and vibrant idea because in one, we are constantly pushing to "sustain the plateau", but the other implies pushing to *exceed* our plateau. (Insert beautiful model and subliminal messaging.) And, just to keep us all clear, our plateau is our potential at that given moment in time. From relationships to a Twinkie, everything has a life span that has a countdown as soon as it is created. Some things may last longer than others (i.e. Twinkie), but our goal is to *thrive*, not survive. Nobody got time for putting in a ton of work just to be in the same exact place. If we have to put the work in anyway then we might as well consistently make it better, right?

Discover New Ways to be Significant:

Piggybacking on our desire to ignore maintaining our achievements, but maintaining our *efforts* to achieve instead, the best way to do so is by discovering new ways to be significant. What must be recognized in this discussion is how we need to focus on being significant in the little things just as much as we will with the bigger ones. We try so hard to make monstrous moves that we lose sight of how big the smaller ones can be. If we want to be more significant in people's lives, opening a door for someone is just as big as coaching the up and coming star. Working *with* your employees is just as important as giving a helping hand. The efforts that most people do not pay attention to are the ones that uphold our character. If we want to make this world a better place then we should always be looking for ways to do so, no matter the scale others perceive them to be. *Everything* is a big thing since it is a purposeful one. The shift here is with our attention. If we discover opportunities to be significant then we discover opportunities to maintain the potential in our character. Little hinges swing big doors.

Those who do not practice a life of purpose and significance tend to look at maintenance as a requirement only when things go wrong. The maintenance team in most companies can replace their name to be the service and repair team. We like to reach a certain position and then walk away from it all until something breaks down and needs "maintenance." Our focus is on making things better, not preventing them from getting worse. If we are trying to prevent them from getting worse then we already have allowed it to be less than what it was. If we are concentrating on making things better then there is no possible way there can be a decline. This shift will assure our continual growth in our purpose and will definitely keep our performance at a very high level. The goal is to perform at a higher level and to exceed our potential.

Our spiritual behavior is what connects us to the world around us and is the separation between success and significance.

All of this goodness in performance and significance is the stuff behind the stuff that makes us purposeful. By doing these things, behind the scenes, we are giving ourselves the chance to be more and do more in order to help this world reach new heights. High performance means doing things that most do not do. Most of us do not prepare on a day-to-day basis. Most of us never evaluate our lives unless the HR department forces us to. Making an impact in every possible moment takes effort that most are not willing to invest in. Reverberation is what creates the domino effect and how one can turn into many. Following up and opening up requires empathy and selflessness. It is in that atmosphere we can really help people as we first understand them and then give them the freedom to use all of *their* assets for *their* growth to excel in *their* purpose.

Resting, although high performers may look at it as the black sheep of the bunch, is what encourages our capabilities to maintain upward trajectory, especially because that is *a lot* of stuff to keep consistent. Besides, if what you do is who you are then there really is no such thing as an off day. It is a lot of work, but the results are priceless and our significance will last this generation and the generations to come.

Commencement

As I said earlier, the definition of commencement is beginning. I prefer to use that word instead of conclusion because although this is the end of this book, it is not the end of *yours*. I believe there is going to be a ridiculous amount of opportunity and prosperity coming your way due to the fact that you did not only read this book, but because you are working on implementing the lessons from it into your daily life. The reason why I know this will happen is because I have been praying for *you* throughout the process of me writing. My hope that this lands in the hands that need it most is so there can be a movement of change for our society. With so much negativity happening around us, I believe it is time for those capable of significance to go out and have the courage to be positive. "To him that knoweth do to good and doeth it not, to him it is sin"(James 4:17). It is our duty to do good once we have learned to be better. Doing *everything* in your power to exceed your potential is now a requirement for you (sorry, not sorry). Speaking of potential, do you know how much I *despise* that word? Growing up, that seemed to be the recurring word used to describe me. I thought that it was a compliment back then, but it could not be more of the opposite. I forget who said this, but potential is a word only used when something does not live up to its expectations. In essence, it defines those that do not render their best. This is why I spoke about *exceeding* your potential. I do not want you to just meet people's expectations. Greatness does not come from doing what is expected. Significance does not happen when people can anticipate what is to come next. Exceeding your potential is how you raise the bar. It is how you challenge not only yourself, but also others to perform at a higher level. In doing so, the word potential will never be used to describe you. Discover your purpose. Work on your mental, physical, and spiritual behavior. Mind. Body. Soul. Remember why you were created and always do the best you can to be selfless. Have faith in your calling and make it your priority. Be engaged and always strive to be more than you are. I have one more story:

My moment of significance occurred not too long ago. My father and I went to a conference. We all understand that my father is a phenomenal man that started medical school and his first church at the age of nineteen. He has worked for some of the biggest hospitals and companies known in health care. He has traveled around the world helping others by healing their body and spirit. But when I had the opportunity to impact his life. When God gave me the gift to give back to him by taking him to an event that helped change his life and forward his progression in his purpose, I realized that my life of significance had begun. I am trying to fight the tears at this very moment just speaking about it so you can imagine how I was when I saw his face light up in pride as I was speaking to a room full of people the same way I am speaking to you now. That was the greatest thing to happen to me. Your moment will be the greatest thing to happen to you. You will know when it comes and there will be an overwhelming emotion of joy when it does because that is when you will realize that you did not meet your potential. You exceeded it.

CPSIA information can be obtained
at www.ICGtesting.com
Printed in the USA
BVOW11s0727140516
447596BV00002B/2/P